Fat-Free & Easy

Great Meals in Minutes!

No Added Fat
No Cholesterol
No Animal Ingredients

Other Books by Jennifer Raymond:

The Best of Jenny's Kitchen
The Peaceful Palate

Fat-Free
& Easy

Great Meals in Minutes!

No Added Fat
No Cholesterol
No Animal Ingredients

Jennifer Raymond

Heart & Soul Publications
1418 Cedar Street
Calistoga, California 94515

Library of Congress Cataloging-in-Publication Data

Raymond, Jennifer
Fat-Free & Easy : great meals in minutes / by Jennifer Raymond.
          p.   9m
Includes index.
ISBN 1-57067-041-2
1. Vegetarian cookery. 2. Low-fat diet--Recipes. 3. Quick and
easy cookery.   I. Title.
TX837.R3796   1997
641.5'638--dc21

                                                    96-54488
                                                    CIP

MacDine Perfect was used to determine nutrient content of the recipes. Figures are rounded to the nearest whole number, which may result in a slight discrepancy between grams of fat and percent of calories from fat. If a range is given for the amount of an ingredient, the analysis is based on an average of the figures given, and ingredients with no measurement are not included in the analysis. Nutritional content may vary depending on specific brands or ingredients used.

*This book is dedicated to the many people
who have made it possible.*

Special thanks to:

*Stephen Avis, my Partner in Life,
who believes in me, encourages me,
and is a faithful recipe taster.*

*Adrien Avis, my Mother by Marriage,
who is always ready to help.*

*Cheryl Woodward, my Beloved Friend,
who is always willing to listen,
and whom I have never inspired to cook.*

Table of Contents

Introduction

*"Your choice of diet can influence your long-term health prospects
more than any other action you might take."*
                                        C. Everett Koop, M.D.
                                        Former U.S. Surgeon General

Ah, the pleasures of fat! It gives food that melt-in-your mouth quality.
It makes meat tender, pastries flaky, sauces smooth, and desserts rich.
It makes food, quite literally, to die for.

And die we do. Heart disease, adult-onset diabetes, high blood pressure,
stroke, colon cancer, and breast cancer lead the list of diseases which
are caused, in large part, by our fondness for fat. All are major killers in
the United States, so common in fact that we tend to think of them as
an inevitable part of aging. Yet, they are not inevitable. In parts of the
world where consumption of fat—particularly animal fat—is low, these
diseases are rare. In Japan, for example, where the traditional diet is
very low in fat, heart disease and breast cancer have been virtually
unknown. As the Japanese adopt Western-style, high-fat diets,
however, the incidence of these diseases is increasing dramatically.

Fat accounts for one third to one half of the calories in the typical
American diet. Although some fat is necessary to supply fat-soluble
vitamins and essential fatty acids, the amount required to meet these
needs is very small. No pure-fat foods such as oil, butter, or margarine
are necessary to meet these requirements. A diet of whole foods that
includes grains, beans, vegetables, and fruits will easily meet your needs.

Some sources of fat are obvious: butter, margarine, oils, mayonnaise,
salad dressings, pastries and deep fried foods. Yet, the majority of fat in
the U.S. diet is hidden in meats, dairy products, and eggs, the very foods
most people think of as healthful.

Consider the following:
- Fifty to seventy percent of the calories in red meat come from fat. Even with the visible fat trimmed off, substantial amounts remain marbled throughout the meat.
- Chicken, which many people think of as low in fat, gets fifty percent of its calories from fat. Even with the skin removed, thirty-five percent of the calories come from fat.
- Eggs derive sixty-five to seventy percent of their calories from fat. To make matters worse, in addition to all its fat, a single egg contains 275 milligrams of cholesterol! The American Heart Association recommends a maximum of 300 milligrams of cholesterol per day, and many health experts feel that even this amount is too high.
- Fat accounts for seventy to ninety percent of the calories in cheese. Cheddar cheese, for example, gets seventy-four percent of its calories from fat while ninety percent of the calories in cream cheese come from fat.
- Over fifty percent of the calories in whole milk come from fat. Even "low-fat" milk (2% milk) gets thirty-five percent of its calories from fat.

If the *amount* of fat in these foods doesn't stop you dead in your tracks, the *type* of fat will. Animal foods contain primarily saturated fat which raises the level of cholesterol in your blood and significantly increases your risk for developing atherosclerosis and heart disease. Add to this the substantial amounts of cholesterol contained in all animal-origin foods (including poultry, fish, and seafood) and it becomes clear why a person eating a typical American diet is so likely to develop heart disease.

Plant-based foods, with just a few exceptions, are significantly lower in fat than animal-origin foods, and most of the fat they contain is the unsaturated variety, which actually lowers blood cholesterol levels. Furthermore, plant foods contain absolutely no cholesterol. The easiest and most effective way to reduce your intake of fat is to switch to a plant-based diet of grains, vegetables, legumes, and fruits. By replacing animal foods with plant foods, your intake of fat will automatically decline, and your consumption of complex carbohydrates and fiber will increase. As a result, you will feel better, constipation will no longer be a problem, and you will lose excess weight without ever going hungry.

The purpose of this book is to provide you with recipes for delicious, nutritionally-balanced meals that can be easily prepared with no added fat. The ingredients are, as much as possible, available in standard supermarkets. Those which might be unfamiliar to you are described in a glossary which precedes the recipes.

Although I have attempted to make the recipes as simple as possible, in the beginning, you may find that you are spending more time in the kitchen than you are used to. Like any new skill, healthful cooking requires some time and practice. However, as you become familiar with the ingredients and the techniques, the time you spend will decrease. Many people find that they actually begin to enjoy food preparation more than they ever have before. Working with beautiful fresh ingredients, preparing meals which are delicious as well as healthful, can be a real inspiration.

If you are under the impression that eliminating fat means eliminating flavor, you are in for some wonderful surprises. Nothing could be farther from the truth. Whole grains, legumes, fresh vegetables and fruits—the basis of fat-free cuisine—provide a remarkable and mouthwatering variety of flavors and textures. The recipes in this book will help you begin enjoying them.

Jennifer Raymond
Calistoga, California
April, 1997

Health Consequences of High-Fat Diets

"The diet which affluent people generally consume is everywhere associated with a similar disease pattern—high rates of heart disease, certain forms of cancer, diabetes, and obesity. These are the major cause of death and disability in the United States . . . The question to be asked, therefore, is not why should we change our diet but why not? What are the risks . . . ? There are none that can be identified and important benefits can be expected."

> D. M. Hegsted, M.D.
> Harvard School of Public Health

Americans—rich and poor alike—consume about forty percent of their calories from fat each day. The health consequences of this high fat consumption are devastating.

Obesity

The most obvious problem associated with consuming a high-fat diet is unwanted weight gain. More than one third of all adults and children in the United States are significantly overweight, and as a result, at increased risk for developing heart disease, stroke, certain cancers, adult-onset diabetes, and a host of other diseases. The majority of overweight adults are unable to lose weight and keep it off. Dieting is notoriously unsuccessful because a diet is a temporary way of eating and any weight loss is likewise temporary.

Permanent weight loss requires a permanent change in eating habits. Reducing the fat in your diet is a permanent change you can live with. **Reducing the fat in your diet allows you to reduce your calorie intake without reducing the amount of food you are eating**. Thus, you are not limited to tiny portions or special foods. You can eat to satisfaction and still lose weight.

There are a number of reasons why high-fat diets are so fattening. To begin with, **fat has more than twice as many calories as either carbohydrate or protein**. A gram of fat contains **nine** calories, while a gram of protein or carbohydrate contains only **four** calories. If your diet is high in fat, you are forced to limit yourself to very small portions to avoid consuming too many calories. Furthermore, dietary fat is much more easily converted to body fat than protein or carbohydrate. The composition of dietary fat is similar to body fat and it takes very little energy for the body to process it for storage. In other words, fat contains more calories than protein and carbohydrate, *and* those calories are converted to body fat much more easily.

By contrast, when your diet is made up of low-fat plant foods you can eat generous, satisfying amounts without gaining weight. Permanent weight loss does not mean eating less, but rather, eating differently. By reducing your intake of fatty foods and replacing them with foods which are high in complex carbohydrates you will lose weight and keep it off without going hungry.

Heart disease

"To build a stone wall, you must have stones. To build coronary artery disease, you must have fat and cholesterol."

Caldwell B. Esselstyn, M.D.

Heart disease is the number one killer of both men and women in the United States. More Americans die from heart disease than from all other causes combined. It is well established that consumption of saturated fat and cholesterol raises blood cholesterol levels and promotes the development of atherosclerosis and heart disease. Saturated fat is solid at room temperature and found primarily in animal-origin foods like meat, poultry, dairy products, and eggs. Cholesterol is found *only* in animal-origin foods. Most people are surprised to learn that poultry and many types of fish contain as much cholesterol as red meat. By eliminating animal foods from your diet, your consumption of saturated fat and cholesterol will decline and with it your risk for heart disease.

The American Heart Association has recommended that no more than thirty percent of each day's calories come from fat. Yet many studies have shown that even this level is too high. In a study reported in the July, 1990 issue of the *Lancet,* Dean Ornish, M.D. found that limiting fat to thirty percent of calories had no effect on reversing heart disease, while a reduction to ten percent of calories made a significant difference.

Cancer

"Eating less fat can reduce the risk of colon, prostate, and breast cancer."
National Research Council, "Diet and Health"

Several types of cancer are more common among populations who
consume a high fat diet. These include cancer of the colon, breast, and
prostate. Unlike heart disease, which is linked to saturated fat, cancer
seems to be linked to *total* fat intake. In other words, consuming a high
fat diet increases your risk for developing these cancers, regardless of
the type of fat you eat.

Hypertension

Commonly known as high blood pressure, hypertension afflicts
approximately 58 million Americans—more than one-fifth of the U.S.
population! Of these, 39 million are under the age of 65. Known as "the
silent killer," hypertension has no symptoms as it damages the arteries,
leading to heart disease, kidney disease, and stroke. Although the exact
causes of hypertension are unknown, many people who are diagnosed
with it are overweight, and in many cases the condition disappears when
the excess weight is lost. The most effective way to lose weight
permanently is by reducing your fat intake.

Adult-Onset Diabetes

Originally thought to be a disease of carbohydrate metabolism, adult-
onset diabetes is now known to be linked to fat consumption as well.
Overweight individuals are at much greater risk for developing this
disease, and when excess weight is lost, the symptoms often disappear.
Once again, the way to lose weight and keep it off is to get the fat out of
your diet.

How Much Fat Should You Eat?

While there is widespread agreement about the detrimental effects of high fat diets, recommendations concerning the maximum amount of fat that should be consumed vary significantly. The American Heart Association, American Cancer Society, and the U.S. Dietary Goals recommend that Americans consume no more than thirty percent of each day's calories from fat. This recommendation is based on what these organizations consider to be a feasible goal. They do not believe that Americans will accept a diet that is lower in fat so they do not recommend it. Yet substantial research indicates that reducing fat to thirty percent of calories does nothing to prevent heart disease, cancer, or other diseases that are caused by our high-fat lifestyle. In order to make a significant difference, fat must be reduced to between ten and twenty percent of calories.

Dean Ornish, M.D. studied individuals with heart disease and found that those who followed the American Heart Association guidelines showed no improvement, and in fact got worse. By contrast, individuals who reduced their fat intake to ten percent of calories showed dramatic improvement, including reduction of blockages in their arteries. This information is thoroughly documented by in his scientific writings in the British medical journal *Lancet,* as well as in his book *Dr. Dean Ornish's Program for Reversing Heart Disease* (Random House, 1990).

Numerous other studies have compared the health of populations that consume high fat diets with those that consume low-fat diets. These studies consistently show lower rates of heart disease and the other "diseases of affluence" in populations that consume very low-fat diets. Dr. T. Colin Campbell of Cornell University studied the diets and health of 6,500 Chinese in mainland China and concluded that in order to have a beneficial impact on health, fat must be reduced to less than twenty percent of daily calories, and ideally to ten percent.

The following table indicates the maximum number of grams of fat you should consume to keep your intake to 10 or 20 percent of daily calories.

Maximum Grams of Fat for Low-fat Diets

	10 percent	20 percent
female	20 grams of fat	40 grams of fat
male	30 grams of fat	60 grams of fat

The chart shows that to limit fat intake to ten percent of calories, a woman should eat no more than 20 grams of fat in a day, and a man should consume no more than 30 grams.

Another method for determining the maximum grams of fat you should consume in a day is to divide your **ideal** weight by six. The result is the maximum grams of fat which should be consumed on a diet which gets ten percent of its calories from fat. Dividing your ideal weight by three will tell you the maximum grams of fat which can be consumed on a diet which gets twenty percent of calories from fat.

At this point, the question usually arises, "But don't I need some fat in my diet?" Indeed, some fat is necessary to supply fat soluble vitamins and essential fatty acids. However, all foods naturally contain some fat, and all of the fat you need is easily provided by a diet of whole foods. There is no nutritional need to consume any pure fats or high fat foods.

Calculating Your Fat Intake

The easiest way to reduce your fat intake is to consume a plant-based diet of whole grains, legumes (dried beans, peas, and lentils), vegetables and fruits. If you stick to these foods and don't add refined fats such as oil or margarine, your consumption of fat will automatically decrease. The beauty of this way of eating is that it eliminates the need to count calories, fat grams, or fat calories.

If, however, knowing the numbers makes you feel more secure, there are several ways to calculate the amount of fat in your diet. Those most commonly used are:

- **Grams of fat**
- **Percentage of calories from fat**
- **Percentage of weight from fat**

Each of these is discussed below. The first two are useful for determining how much fat your diet contains. The third, though widely used by food manufacturers and advertisers, is virtually useless.

Grams of Fat

A gram is a measurement of weight (28.5 grams = 1 ounce). To determine the number of fat grams you are consuming, simply add the grams of fat in all of the foods you eat in a day. These will be listed on the labels of prepared foods. For foods without labels, you will need to refer to a table of nutrient values, which can be purchased in most bookstores.

Percentage of Calories from Fat

The percentage of calories from fat enables you to evaluate foods in relation to your dietary goals. For example, if your goal is to limit calories from fat to ten percent of your diet, then most of the foods you consume should get ten percent (or fewer) calories from fat. Percentage of calories from fat can be misleading, however, when evaluating foods that are high in sugar. Since sugar contributes a lot of calories, the percentage of calories from fat may be quite low in a high-sugar food, even though the quantity of fat (grams of fat) in the food is quite high.

To calculate the percentage of calories from fat in a food:

1. Determine the grams of fat in one serving of the food.
2. Multiply grams of fat by nine to determine the fat calories.
3. Divide the fat calories by the total calories in one serving.
4. Multiply by 100 to get the percentage of calories from fat.

Consider, for example, a food containing 4 grams of fat and 200 calories:

$$4 \times 9 = 36 \text{ fat calories}$$
$$36 \div 200 = .18 \times 100 = 18\% \text{ of calories from fat}$$

Percentage of Weight from Fat

This is a measurement of the amount of weight of a food that is contributed by fat. Manufacturers love to use this measurement in their advertising because it makes the fat content appear lower than it actually is. This is because most of the weight in any food comes from water and the weight contributed by fat is very small by comparison. Thus, when the weight of fat is divided by the total weight of the food, the percentage will be very small even though the fat content may be high.

Consider the following example: low-fat milk is advertised as "2% milk," because two percent of the total weight of the milk comes from fat (most of the weight of milk is water). Yet, an eight-ounce glass of low-fat milk contains almost five grams of fat and 121 calories. Fully *thirty-five percent* of the calories in low-fat milk come from fat!

Don't feel alone if you've been fooled by this deceptive marketing tactic. Even the U.S. government has been mislead. The U.S. Department of Agriculture Commodities Program, which supplies food for 92 million school lunches each day, advertises its beef patties as being less than twenty-four percent fat, when in actuality, 64 percent of the calories come from fat. It's no wonder that a third of our nation's schoolchildren are overweight!

Do not be misled by the low-fat claims of manufacturers. Use the grams of fat or the percentage of calories from fat to determine how much fat is in your food. Or better yet, stick to a plant-based diet without added fats and forget about the numbers!

Sources of Fat in Food

Most of the fat in the U.S. diet comes from meats, dairy products, and eggs, the very foods which most people think of as healthful. Red meat, for example, derives fifty to seventy percent of its calories from fat. Even with the visible fat trimmed off, substantial amounts of fat remain marbled throughout the meat. The amount of fat in some commonly consumed animal foods is listed below.

Fat Content of Animal Foods

Food	Percent of calories from fat
butter, lard	100%
bacon	90%
cream cheese	87%
hot dog	85%
half and half	80%
hard cheese (cheddar, muenster, jack)	70-75%
red meat	50-80%
ice cream	65%
whole eggs	64%
salmon	60%
tuna salad	55%
whole milk	50%
turkey, dark meat (with skin)	47%
chicken with skin	45%
tuna in oil	40%
turkey, white meat (with skin)	38%
low-fat milk (2% milk)	35%
turkey, dark meat (without skin)	35%
chicken (without skin)	32%
low-fat yogurt	22%
turkey, white meat (without skin)	19%
low-fat cottage cheese	18%
tuna in water	14%
nonfat milk/nonfat yogurt	3-5%

It is easy to see that the majority of animal foods exceed twenty percent of calories from fat. By replacing animal foods with plant foods—grains, beans, vegetables and fruits—your intake of fat will automatically decline, and your consumption of complex carbohydrate will increase. The following table shows the fat content of a variety of plant foods.

Fat Content of Plant Foods

Food	Percent of calories from fat
nuts (except chestnuts)	85 to 90%
olives	80%
avocado	76%
tofu	50%
reduced fat tofu	28%
oatmeal	16%
corn	10%
whole wheat bread	10%
broccoli	9%
chestnuts	7%
polenta	6%
brown rice	5%
carrot	5%
sweet potato, yam	4%
pasta	4%
black beans	4%
lentils	4%
pinto beans	3%
orange	2%
banana	2%
potato	2%

As you can see, most plant foods easily meet the criteria of twenty percent or fewer calories from fat. The exceptions are nuts and seeds (including nut and seed butters), avocados, olives, and tofu. It is also interesting to note that foods like pasta and potatoes, which have been frequently condemned as "fattening," are actually extremely low in fat. It is the high fat foods we serve them with, like butter, cheese, and sour cream which add excessive calories and cause the problem.

Fats Are Not Created Equal

Another difference between animal foods and plant foods is the type of fat they contain. Animal foods are high in **saturated fat**, which is solid at room temperature and is known to raise blood cholesterol levels. Some examples are butter, lard, and the fat in meat and cheese.

By contrast, plant foods contain mostly **unsaturated fats** which are liquid at room temperature and which have been shown to lower blood cholesterol levels. This is undoubtedly part of the reason why vegetarians have lower rates of heart disease than meat-eaters. However, consuming large amounts of unsaturated fats has negative health consequences as well, including excess calories and unwanted weight gain as well as increased incidence of certain cancers.

One other group of fats that you should be aware of are **hydrogenated fats**. These are liquid fats which have been made solid by the process of hydrogenation. Two common examples are margarine and vegetable shortening. Hydrogenation turns liquid (unsaturated) fats into solid fats. These chemically hardened fats affect the arteries in the same way that saturated fats do. In addition, hydrogenation causes the formation of substances called *trans-fatty acids* which are known to be detrimental to health.

Cholesterol is a fat-like substance found *only* in animal foods. Consumption of cholesterol can raise blood cholesterol levels and increase the risk of heart disease. By eliminating animal foods, you completely remove cholesterol from your diet. Your body will manufacture any cholesterol that it needs.

Tips for Cutting the Fat

By now it should be clear that meat, dairy products, and eggs are the major sources of fat in the typical U.S. diet. Switching to a plant-based diet is the first step you should take to reduce your fat consumption. The following tips will help you reduce your fat intake even further.

- Avoid fried foods, deep-fried foods, and fat-laden pastries. Check your market for low-fat and no-fat alternatives.

- Baking, grilling, and oven-roasting are great alternatives to frying.

- Don't sauté: **liquid-braise** instead! Heat approximately 1/2 cup of liquid (water, wine, vegetable stock, dry sherry) in a large pot or skillet. Add the ingredients to be braised and cook over high heat, stirring occasionally, until tender. This will take about five minutes. Add small amounts of additional liquid if the food begins to stick.

- The **braise-deglaze** technique allows you to actually caramelize onions, bringing out all their natural flavor and sweetness with no added fat. This is especially useful in the preparation of soups and sauces. Heat about 1/2 cup of water in a skillet and add the onions. Cook over high heat until the water has evaporated and browned bits of onion begin to stick to the pan. Add another 1/4 cup of water, stirring to loosen any stuck particles. Continue cooking, stirring occasionally, until the water has again evaporated. Repeat this process until the onions are nicely browned. This will take about 30 minutes.

- Add onions and garlic to soups and stews at the beginning of the cooking time so their flavors will mellow without sautéing.

- When oil is absolutely necessary to prevent sticking, lightly apply a vegetable oil spray.

- Use nonstick pots and pans which allow foods to be prepared with no added fat.

- Use nonstick pans or a microwave oven to reheat foods.

- Use a fat-free dressing on salads. Several commercial varieties are available, or try the recipes on pages 64 to 66.

- Seasoned rice vinegar and balsamic vinegar make great fat-free salad dressings.

- Replace the oil in salad dressing recipes with seasoned rice vinegar, vegetable stock, bean cooking liquid, or with water. For a thicker dressing, try the following:
  > Combine 1 tablespoon of cornstarch with 1 cup of water in a small pan and whisk smooth. Heat, stirring constantly, until thick and clear. Refrigerate. Use in place of oil in any salad dressing. May be kept refrigerated for up to three weeks.

- Instead of topping vegetables with butter or fat-laden sauces, try lemon juice, seasoned rice vinegar, or a fat-free salad dressing.

- Make soup thick and creamy by adding mashed potatoes or quick-cooking rolled oats. For soups which will be pureed, simply cook and puree diced potatoes along with the other ingredients. For other soups, add instant mashed potato flakes or quick-cooking rolled oats which have been pureed with a small amount of liquid.

- Limit your consumption of avocados, olives, nuts and seeds, and coconut, which are all high in fat.

- Select baked versions of fried foods, like tortilla chips and potato chips.

- Baked pretzels make a great fat-free snack food.

- Avoid deep-fried foods like French fries. Try Oven Fries (page 98) instead.

- Replace ice cream with fruit sorbet or a frozen fruit freeze (page 134).

- The amount of fat in baked goods can often be reduced with no noticeable change in taste or texture. Experiment with your recipes, adding a bit less fat each time, and evaluating the results. You may have to add a bit of extra liquid to achieve the desired consistency.

- Applesauce, mashed banana, prune puree, or canned pumpkin may be substituted for fat in many baked goods with a bit of experimentation.

- Prepare pies with a single crust to reduce fat and calories (about 100 fewer calories per serving).

- Crumb crusts may be prepared with less fat than pastry crusts.

Meeting Your Protein Needs

The average American undoubtedly considers protein to be the most important of all nutrients. In fact, most Americans believe their diets to be satisfactory as long as they are getting enough protein, and to this end, consume large quantities of meat, dairy products, and eggs each day. It is true that these foods provide substantial protein. However, they are also extremely high in fat. In fact, most of them contain more calories from fat than from protein! It is these foods which account for much of the fat in the typical, high-fat, American diet.

The real irony is that consuming of large amounts of protein, which costs so dearly in terms of fat intake, is totally unnecessary, because the human protein requirement is surprisingly small. While protein is indeed necessary for the body's growth, repair and maintenance, only ten percent of each day's calories need to come from protein. All plant foods, with the exception of fruit, contain at least this amount of protein, and a diet based on a variety of plant foods easily supplies human protein needs. The following table shows the protein requirement for individuals of different ages.

Average Protein Requirement in Grams

Age	Protein Requirement
Children 1-10 years	16-28 g
Females 11-24 25+	44-46 g 46-50 g
Males 11-24 25+	45-59 g 63 g

These protein requirements, which have been determined by the Food and Nutrition Board of the National Research Council, contain generous margins of safety to cover individual differences which might affect protein needs. Thus, these amounts are sufficient for athletes and other physically active individuals, as well as for those who are less active. These requirements are easily met with a low-fat, plant-based diet, as is illustrated by the following one-day menu:

Protein Supplied by a One-day Plant-Based Diet

Breakfast	Protein
1 cup cooked oatmeal	7 g
1 cup soy milk	6 g
1/2 grapefruit	1 g
	14 grams
Lunch	
1 cup split pea soup	9 g
2 slices whole wheat bread	5 g
2 tablespoons hummus	2 g
1 cup green salad	1 g
2 pumpkin raisin cookies	3 g
	20 grams
Snack	
1 bowl quick pasta salad	7 g
	7 grams
Dinner	
1 vegetarian burger patty	12 g
1 burger bun	5 g
3/4 cup Oven Fries	2 g
3/4 cup steamed broccoli	4 g
1 serving berry cobbler	3 g
	26 grams
Total protein:	**67 grams**

It should be mentioned that the above menu represents a fairly modest food intake (just over 1500 calories). Most adolescents and many adults eat more food than this in a day, which further increases their protein intake. Yet even this rather modest diet supplies 67 grams of protein, more than enough to meet the needs of individuals of all ages, and this protein is supplied without the excessive fat and cholesterol found in animal foods.

It should also be noted that no complicated mixing or matching of foods is required to meet your protein needs on a plant-based diet. Many people are under the impression that foods need to be carefully combined at every meal in order to get complete, high-quality protein. However, this notion, called "protein complementarity" is no longer considered necessary by nutrition professionals. In their 1993 Position Paper on Vegetarian Diets, the American Dietetic Association stated: "Conscious combining of [plant] foods, as the complementary protein dictum suggests, is unnecessary." Simply eating a variety of grains, beans, vegetables, and fruits each day will supply your body with all the protein it needs.

Problems with Excess Protein

As mentioned above, the human protein requirement is surprisingly small. Most Americans, consuming a diet based on animal foods, eat two to three times more protein than they need each day. In the process, they consume excessive quantities of saturated fat and cholesterol, known risk factors for heart disease. In addition, research has shown that *animal proteins* also raise blood cholesterol levels, further contributing to the development of heart disease. No such link has been demonstrated between plant proteins and heart disease.

High protein diets also increase the risk of developing kidney disease and osteoporosis. When excess protein is consumed, the kidneys are overworked as they labor to eliminate the surplus. In the process, calcium is removed from the bones and excreted in the urine. Much of this lost calcium is never replaced, because the body is unable to absorb calcium fast enough to replenish the losses. In other words, eating calcium-rich foods and taking calcium supplements cannot compensate for the calcium losses which result from a high protein diet. Thus, an individual on a high protein diet is constantly losing more calcium from the bones than is being replaced, eventually leading to weakening of the bones and osteoporosis. *One of the best ways to prevent osteoporosis is to decrease your protein intake. The easiest way to do this is to shift to a plant-based diet.*

Protein Myths and Facts

Myth:*We need a lot of protein to be healthy.*
Fact: While it is true that protein is essential, the amount we need each day is quite small: about ten percent of each day's calories. Most Americans consume significantly more protein than they need each day.

Myth:*Protein is only found in animal foods: meat, dairy, and eggs.*
Fact: Protein is found in all non-junk foods. Grains, beans, vegetables and fruits all contain protein. Eating a variety of these supplies plenty of protein, without the saturated fat and cholesterol of animal protein sources.

Myth:*Eating a lot of protein provides the body with a margin of safety.*
Fact: Eating excess protein provides no margin of safety because the body cannot store protein. When you eat more protein than you need, the body simply converts it to fat or burns it for energy. Furthermore, consumption of excess protein overworks the liver and kidneys, and causes the body to excrete calcium, leading to osteoporosis.

Myth: *Getting enough protein without meat requires careful planning.*
Fact: Plant-based diets easily supply plenty of protein, without any complicated planning or food combining. Simply eat a variety of grains, beans, vegetables, and fruits each day.

Myth:*Athletes need extra protein.*
Fact: While athletes may require slightly more protein than sedentary individuals, that amount is easily met by consumption of a normal diet. The protein requirement set by the U.S. government is purposely high to cover the requirements of athletes and others performing strenuous activities. Athletes need more calories, to cover their increased energy output, and these calories should come from carbohydrate, the body's perfect energy food.

Myth:*A vegetarian diet may be fine for adults, but children need meat.*
Fact: Like adults, children can easily get all the protein they need on a vegetarian diet, and they will have a significantly lower risk for developing heart disease, certain cancers, obesity, and adult-onset diabetes later in life.

Salt

Although salt has not been shown to cause hypertension (high blood pressure), it is known to exacerbate the condition in salt-sensitive individuals. High salt intake has also been implicated as a cause of stomach cancer, and has been shown to increase calcium losses from the bones, increasing the risk of osteoporosis.

Average salt consumption in the United States is between 6,000 and 10,000 milligrams each day. The recommended maximum intake is between 2,000 and 3,000 milligrams daily. Much of the salt we consume is "hidden" in processed foods. More is added in cooking and at the table.

Our taste for salty foods is acquired, and just we have "learned" to like salty foods, our tastes can be retrained to appreciate the true flavors of food without the overbearing flavor of salt. Begin by progressively decreasing the amount of salt you use in cooking. For example, if a recipe calls for a teaspoon of salt, reduce it to 3/4 teaspoon, then to 1/2 teaspoon, and so forth. As you gradually reduce the amount of salt you add to cooked foods, your taste for salt will diminish quite painlessly.

A number of sodium-free seasoning mixes are available to help you add flavor without adding salt. These come in shaker bottles, ready to put on the table in place of the salt shaker. Many unsalted snack foods are also available, though you should be sure your selection is also low in fat.

The recipes in this book have been designed with the goal of reducing salt; however, it has not been eliminated altogether. In the big health picture, reducing fat is the highest priority and a bit of salt in fat-free food is often the key to making it acceptable to the average American palate. If you do not use salt, simply eliminate it from the recipes. It is only there to add flavor. Whenever possible, I have specified "salt to taste" at the end of a recipe. Depending on the other ingredients in a recipe and your own tastes, you may find that no salt is required. I would also suggest the use of reduced-sodium soy sauce wherever soy sauce is specified. Look for it in your supermarket or natural foods store.

Menu Planning

Menu planning can save you time and money, and insure that you will have delicious fat-free meals.

- You'll save **shopping time** by getting all your ingredients in a single shopping trip.

- You'll save **cooking time** because needed ingredients will be on hand and the food you prepare food can be part of several meals.

- You'll save **money** by purchasing less expensive ingredients and fewer prepared foods. Also, you'll probably find yourself eating at home more often.

Menu planning doesn't require that you figure out a complete set of menus for each and every meal. Since the foods we eat for breakfast tend to be similar from day to day, you simply need to include some of these foods on your shopping list: whole grain breads, cereals, fresh fruit. Lunches may also be similar from day to day, or can incorporate dinner leftovers which are easily reheated in a microwave oven. Even dinners don't require a separate menu each and every night if you prepare large enough quantities so that you have leftovers for a second (or even a third) meal.

I also like to incorporate what I call "progressive meals" into my menu planning. For example, the first night, I might cook a double batch of pinto beans and brown rice for "Rice and Beans with Greens" (page 113). The following night, I use the leftover cooked beans to make "Quick Chili Beans" (page 116). Then I use the leftover chili beans to make "Chili Corn Pie" (page 117). The preparation of each of these meals takes less time than if I had to begin from scratch each time.

On the following page are the steps I use in my own menu planning.

Menu Planning Guidelines

1. Set aside a bit of time to plan a menu for a week.

2. Look through this book and your favorite recipes and select three
    or four main dishes. Plan to prepare enough of each these to
    provide at least two meals (this will provide all your dinners for
    the week as well as some lunches.

3. Choose two or three grains dishes that can be served with the
    main dishes you've selected. These can be as simple as brown
    rice, pasta, or polenta.

4. Select recipes for a couple of soups or prepared salads (like Pasta
    Salad or Aztec Salad in this book). These keep well and can be
    served with the main dishes you've chosen and also used for
    lunches and snacks.

5. Compile a shopping list of all the ingredients you'll need for the
    recipes you've selected.

6. Add some fresh vegetables and fruits for salads and side dishes.

7. Add foods you'll need for breakfasts and lunches (whole grain
    breads, whole grain cereals, fresh fruits and vegetables).

8. Add any staples you might need to restock, including spices,
    packaged soups, and other ready-to-eat foods. (It's helpful to
    keep a running shopping list on the refrigerator or in some other
    convenient place in the kitchen where these items can be listed as
    soon as you run out or notice that you're getting low on them).

9. Have a bite to eat if you're hungry (never go grocery shopping
    when you're hungry!!!), and you're ready to head to the store.

10. Save your menus and shopping lists. You can reuse them or
    modify them for future menu planning.

Menu Ideas

Breakfasts

Fresh fruits and whole grains are perfect foods for breakfast. Choose from among the following:

cold cereal (should contain no added fat and minimal sugar)
hot cereal: oatmeal, nine-grain, Teff (p. 36), etc.
bagels
whole grain toast
fat-free muffins
Buckwheat Corncakes (p. 30)
Whole Wheat Pancakes (p. 31)
Oatmeal Waffles (p. 32)
fresh fruit including melon, citrus, and berries
Applesauce (p. 37)
Stewed Prunes (p. 37)

Lunches or Light Dinners

Pasta Salad (p. 58)
Creamy Lima Soup (p. 71)

Green Velvet Soup (p. 68) or Split Pea Soup (p. 76)
whole wheat bread
orange slices

Golden Mushroom Soup (p. 78)
spring mix with Fat-Free Vinaigrette (p. 64)
whole grain bread

Aztec Salad (p. 54)
Cornbread (p. 43) or warm corn tortillas
honeydew melon wedges

Missing Egg Salad (p. 47) with pita or whole grain bread
Red Potato Salad (p. 59)
Tomato Soup (p. 69)

Dinners

Pita Pizzas (p. 121)
Minestrone (p. 70)
green salad with Balsamic Vinaigrette (p. 64)

Quick Chili Beans (p. 117) or Spicy Refried Beans (p. 116)
Brown Rice (p. 97) or Spanish Rice (p. 98)
green salad with Fat-Free Vinaigrette (p. 64)

Shepherd's Pie (p. 112)
Wild Basmati Pilaf (p. 99)
Braised Kale or Collards (p. 85)

Autumn Stew (p. 80)
whole grain bread
green salad with Piquant Dressing (p. 66)

Black Bean Soup (p. 73)
Mixed Greens with Quick Piquant Dressing (p. 52)
rye bread

Holiday Tofu Roast (p. 113)
Traditional Bread Dressing (p.103)
Mashed Potatoes & Gravy (p. 104)

Boca Burgers
Oven Fries (p. 89)
corn on the cob
Spinach Salad with Curry Dressing (p. 50)

Crostini with Roasted Red Peppers (p. 45)
Roasted Vegetables with Pasta (p. 110)
Beets with Mustard Dill Dressing (p. 86)

Lentil Barley Stew (p. 82)
Braised Kale (p. 85)
Pumpkin Spice Muffins (p. 40)

Stocking Your Pantry

Keeping some basic ingredients on hand will enable you to prepare delicious, fat-free meals with just a moment's notice.

Produce

yellow onions	carrots
garlic	celery
romaine lettuce	potatoes

Grains

pasta	polenta
rolled oats	couscous
brown rice	bulgur
whole wheat pastry flour	whole wheat flour
unbleached flour	cornmeal
whole grain bread (may be frozen)	
tortillas: corn and whole (may be frozen)	
pita bread (may be frozen)	

Dried Legumes

dried lentils	dried split peas
dried pinto beans	dried black beans

Canned, Frozen, and Prepared Foods

canned beans: black, kidney, garbanzos, etc.
canned tomatoes, tomato sauce, and paste
canned pumpkin
canned or frozen corn
ramen soups, soup cups, and canned soups
canned vegetarian beans:baked, chili, and refried
Boca Burger or other fat-free vegetarian burger
Mori Nu tofu (keeps for 6 months to 12 months)
Dijon-style mustard, ketchup, salsa, soy sauce
dried herbs and spices

Ingredients That May Be New to You

The majority of ingredients in the recipes are common and widely available in grocery stores. A few which may be unfamiliar are described below.

agar — a sea vegetable used as a thickener and gelling agent instead of gelatin which is a slaughterhouse by-product. Available in natural food stores and Asian markets. May also be called "agar agar."

arrowroot — a natural thickener which is may be substituted for cornstarch.

balsamic vinegar — mellow-flavored wine vinegar which is delicious in salad dressings and marinades. Available in most food stores.

Boca Burgers — a fat-free vegetarian burger with a meaty taste and texture, available in natural food stores, usually in the freezer case.

bulgur — hard red winter wheat which has been cracked and toasted. Cooks quickly and has a delicious, nutty flavor. May be sold in supermarkets as "Ala".

couscous — called "Middle Eastern pasta." Made from the same type of wheat as pasta, however the wheat is cracked instead of ground. Available in the grain section of many supermarkets, as well as at natural food stores and ethnic markets.

diced green chilies — refers to diced Anaheim chilies, which are mildly hot. These are available canned (Ortega is one brand) or fresh. When using fresh chilies, remove skin by charring it under a broiler and rubbing it off.

Fat-Free Nayonaise — a fat-free, cholesterol-free mayonnaise substitute which contains no dairy products or eggs.

garlic granules — a granulated form of garlic powder which remains free-flowing.

Harvest Burger for Recipes — ready-to-use, ground beef substitute made from soy. Ideal for tacos, pasta sauces, and chili. Made by Green Giant (Pillsbury) and available in supermarket frozen food sections.

instant bean flakes — precooked black or pinto beans which can be quickly reconstituted with boiling water and used as a side dish, dip, sauce, or burrito filling. Fantastic Foods and Taste Adventure are two brands, available in natural food stores and some supermarkets.

jicama ("hick-ama") — a delicious root vegetable that is a crisp, slightly sweet addition to salads. Usually sold in the unrefrigerated area of your supermarket's produce section.

lite soy sauce — may also be called "reduced-sodium soy sauce." Compare labels to find the brand with the lowest sodium content.

low-sodium baking powder — baking powder made without sodium bicarbonate. Available in natural food stores and some supermarkets.

prewashed salad mix, prewashed spinach — mixtures of lettuce, spinach, and other salad ingredients which have been cleaned and dried. They store well and make salad preparation a snap. Several different mixes are available in the produce department of most food stores. "Spring mix" is particularly flavorful.

prune puree — may also be called "prune butter." Can be used in place of fat in baked goods. Commercial brands are WonderSlim and Lekvar. Prune baby food or pureed stewed prunes may also be used.

red pepper flakes — dried, crushed chili peppers, available in the spice section or with the Mexican foods.

reduced-fat tofu — contains about one third the fat of regular tofu. Three brands are MoriNu Lite, White Wave, and Tree of Life. Sold in natural food stores and supermarkets.

reduced-sodium soy sauce — may also be called "lite soy sauce." Compare labels to find the brand with the lowest sodium content.

rice milk — a beverage made from partially fermented rice which can be used in place of dairy milk on cereal and in most recipes. Available in natural food stores and some supermarkets.

roasted red peppers — roasted red bell peppers. Add great flavor and color to a variety of dishes. Roast your own (page 96) or purchase them already roasted, packed in water, in most grocery stores. Usually located near the pickles.

seasoned rice vinegar — a mild vinegar, seasoned with sugar and salt. Great for salad dressings and on cooked vegetables. Available in most grocery stores with the vinegar or in the Asian Foods section.

seitan ("say-tan") — also called "wheat meat," seitan is a high protein, fat-free food with a meaty texture and flavor. Available in the deli case or freezer of natural food stores.

silken tofu — a smooth, delicate tofu which is excellent for sauces, cream soups, and dips. Often available in special packaging which allows storage without refrigeration for up to a year. Refrigerate after opening. One popular brand, Mori-Nu, is available in most grocery stores. Ask for the reduced fat, "Lite" variety.

soy milk — made from soybeans. Use as a beverage, on cereal, or as a for dairy milk and cream in most recipes. Available in regular, low-fat, fat-free, and calcium-fortified varieties. Available in natural food stores and many supermarkets.

Spike — a seasoning mixture of vegetables and herbs. Comes in a salt-free version, as well as the original version which contains salt. (I used the original version when testing the recipes in this book.) Sold in natural food stores and many supermarkets.

textured vegetable protein (TVP) — meat-like ingredient made from defatted soy flour. Rehydrate with boiling water to add protein and meaty texture to sauces, chili, and stews. One mail-order company, Harvest Direct, sells seasoned varieties, including an excellent burger mix (call 1-800-8FLAVOR to order). TVP is sold in natural food stores.

unbleached flour — white flour which has not been chemically whitened. Available in most grocery stores.

whole wheat pastry flour — milled from soft spring wheat, it retains the bran and germ, and at the same time produces lighter-textured baked goods than regular whole wheat flour. Available in natural food stores.

BREAKFAST FOODS

Start your day with a good breakfast. Whole grain cereals and breads, as well as fat-free muffins, pancakes, and waffles are all good choices. Add a bit of fresh fruit, and you have a meal that will keep you going all morning long.

Tips for Making Perfect Pancakes

- Mix the dry ingredients in one bowl and the liquids in another. Combine them just before cooking, stirring only enough to remove any lumps.

- Use a good-quality nonstick skillet or griddle to minimize the amount of fat needed to prevent the pancakes from sticking.

- Preheat the pan so that sprinkles of water dance on it, but not so hot that it smokes. Mist it with vegetable oil spray to insure that the pancakes can be turned easily.

- Pour a small amount of batter for each cake (smaller cakes are easier to turn), and let it cook until the top is bubbly and the edges are dry.

- Pancakes are best when they are fresh and hot. Try them with fresh fruit, fruit preserves, or with syrup

Buckwheat Corncakes

Makes 16 3-inch pancakes

Buckwheat adds a wonderful, hearty flavor to these easily prepared pancakes. Serve them with homemade applesauce, fresh fruit, or maple syrup.

1/2   **cup buckwheat flour**
1/2   **cup cornmeal**
1/2   **teaspoon baking powder**
1/4   **teaspoon baking soda**
1/4   **teaspoon salt**

1   **ripe banana, mashed**
2   **tablespoons maple syrup**
1   **tablespoon vinegar**
1   **cup soy milk or rice milk**

Stir the buckwheat flour, cornmeal, baking powder, baking soda, and salt together in a mixing bowl.

In a separate bowl, combine the mashed banana, maple syrup, vinegar, and soy milk or rice milk. Add to the flour mixture, stirring just enough to remove any lumps and make a pourable batter. Add a bit more milk if the batter seems too thick.

Preheat a nonstick skillet or griddle, then spray it with a vegetable oil spray. Pour small amounts of batter onto the heated surface and cook until the tops bubble. Turn carefully with a spatula and cook the second sides until golden brown, about 1 minute. Serve immediately.

Per pancake: 43 calories (0% from fat)
               1 g protein; 9 g carbohydrate; 0 g fat; 65 mg sodium; 0 mg cholesterol

Whole Wheat Pancakes

Makes 16 3-inch pancakes

Five simple ingredients are all it takes to make nutritious, whole grain pancakes. Serve them with fresh fruit, unsweetened fruit preserves, or maple syrup.

> 1   **banana**
> 1 1/4 **cups soy milk or rice milk**
> 1   **tablespoon maple syrup**
>
> 1   **cup whole wheat pastry flour or whole wheat flour**
> 2   **teaspoons baking powder**

In a large bowl, mash the banana, then stir in the soy milk or rice milk and maple syrup.

In a separate bowl, mix the flour and baking powder together, then stir them into the banana mixture.

Pour small amounts of the batter onto a preheated nonstick, lightly oil-sprayed griddle or skillet and cook until the tops bubble. Turn with a spatula and cook the second sides until golden brown. Serve at once.

Per pancake: 44 calories (0% from fat)
                    1 g protein; 8 g carbohydrate; 0 g fat; 9 mg sodium; 0 mg cholesterol

Oatmeal Waffles

Makes 4 waffles

Oatmeal waffles are my own personal favorite. They are substantial and chewy, a bit like eating oatmeal with a crunchy crust.

2	**cups rolled oats**
2	**cups water**
1	**banana**
1	**tablespoon sugar or maple syrup**
1/4	**teaspoon salt**
1	**teaspoon vanilla**

Place all the ingredients into a blender and blend until smooth. Pour some of the batter into a preheated, oil-sprayed waffle iron. Cook for 10 minutes without lifting the lid. The cooking time may vary slightly with different waffle irons. Serve with fresh fruit.

Note: The batter should be pourable. If it becomes too thick as it stands, add a bit more water to achieve desired consistency.

Per waffle: 203 calories (14% from fat)
            8 g protein; 33 g carbohydrate; 3 g fat; 134 mg sodium; 0 mg cholesterol

Scrambled Tofu

Serves 4

For a substantial breakfast, try scrambled tofu, which stands in nicely for scrambled eggs. I like to serve this with toasted English muffins, Braised Potatoes (next page), and chutney. The recipe can be embellished with additional vegetables, such as sliced celery, diced zucchini, or grated carrot. Cook these with the onions.

Although tofu contains a moderate amount of fat, the fat it contains is mostly unsaturated. Like other plant-based foods, it contains no cholesterol.

1	**tablespoon soy sauce**
1/2	**medium onion, chopped**
2	**cups sliced mushrooms**
1	**pound firm tofu, diced or crumbled**
1 1/2	**teaspoons curry powder**

Heat 1/2 cup of water and the soy sauce in a large nonstick skillet and cook the onion and mushrooms for 5 minutes. Add the tofu, then stir in the curry powder. Continue cooking until heated throughly, about 5 minutes.

Per serving: 114 calories (24% from fat)
13 g protein; 8 g carbohydrate; 3 g fat; 158 mg sodium; 0 mg cholesterol

Braised Potatoes

Serves 2 to 4

These quick potatoes are delicious with ketchup, barbecue sauce, or chili and spicy salsa. Be sure to use a nonstick skillet.

4   large red or gold potatoes

4   teaspoons soy sauce
1   onion, chopped
1   teaspoon chili powder
  black pepper (optional)

Scrub the potatoes, but do not peel them. Cut them into 1/4-inch thick slices and steam them over boiling water until just tender when pierced with a sharp knife, about 10 minutes.

Heat 1/2 cup of water and the soy sauce in a large nonstick skillet. Add the onion and cook until soft, about 5 minutes. Add the steamed potatoes and chili powder and stir gently to mix. Cook over medium heat, stirring from time to time, for 3 to 5 minutes. Sprinkle with fresh ground black pepper if desired.

Per serving: 200 calories (0% from fat)
               6 g protein; 43 g carbohydrate; 0 g fat; 215 mg sodium; 0 mg cholesterol

Creamy Oatmeal

Makes 3 cups

You'll love this delicious, creamy oatmeal. The vanilla soy milk or rice milk add just a bit of sweetness.

1   **cup quick rolled oats**
21/2   **cups vanilla soy or rice milk**

Combine rolled oats and milk in an uncovered saucepan over medium heat. Bring to a simmer and cook 1 minute. Cover the pan, turn off the heat and let stand 3 minutes.

Per 1/2 cup: 97 calories (17% from fat)
            4 g protein; 17 g carbohydrate; 2 g fat; 46 mg sodium; 0 mg cholesterol

Quick Breakfast Pudding

Makes about 3 cups

This pudding takes about 10 minutes and is like a dessert for breakfast.

8-10 **dried apricot halves**
3-4   **large dried figs**
1/4   **cup raisins**
1   **apple**
1   **cup quick rolled oats**
3   **cups vanilla soy or rice milk**
1/4   **teaspoon cinnamon**

Finely chop the apricots, figs, and raisins in a food processor. Cut the apple and remove the core. Add the apple to the dried fruit in the food processor and chop finely. Transfer the fruit to a saucepan and add the remaining ingredients. Bring to a slow simmer and cook over medium heat until thickened, about 5 minutes. Stir occasionally during cooking.

Per 1/2 cup: 160 calories (12% from fat)
            5 g protein; 30 g carbohydrate; 2 g fat; 47 mg sodium; 0 mg cholesterol

Breakfast Teff

Makes 2 cups

Teff has been a staple grain in northern Africa for centuries, and has recently become available in the United States, to the delight of chefs and nutritionists. This tiny grain is extremely nutritious and makes an absolutely delicious breakfast cereal with a wheat-like flavor. Ask for teff at your favorite natural food store.

1/2   **cup teff**
11/2 **cups water**
1/4   **teaspoon salt (optional)**

soy milk or rice milk for serving

Combine teff and water in a saucepan. Add salt if desired and stir to mix. Cook over low heat, stirring occasionally, until thick, about 15 minutes. Serve with soy milk or rice milk.

Per 1 cup: 200 calories (10% from fat)
            8 g protein; 35 g carbohydrate; 2 g fat; 268 mg sodium; 0 mg cholesterol

Applesauce

Makes 4 cups

Applesauce is so simple to make, and is delicious on toast, pancakes, or on hot cereal. Try it hot or cold.

6   large green apples
1/2-1 cup undiluted apple juice concentrate
1/2   teaspoon cinnamon

Peel the apples if desired, then core and dice them into a large pan. Add enough apple juice concentrate to cover the bottom of the pan, then cover and cook over very low heat until the apples are soft. Mash slightly with a fork if desired, then stir in the cinnamon. Serve hot or cold.

Per 1/2 cup: 60 calories (0% from fat)
0.2 g protein; 14 g carbohydrate; 0 g fat; 3 mg sodium; 0 mg cholesterol

Stewed Prunes

Makes 1 1/2 cups

Prunes are a delicious source of vitamins, minerals and fiber.

1   cup dried prunes

Combine the prunes and 1 cup of water in a saucepan. Cover and simmer until the prunes are soft, about 20 minutes. Serve hot or cold, plain or with soy milk or rice milk.

Per 1/2 cup: 129 calories (0% from fat)
1 g protein; 30 g carbohydrate; 0 g fat; 2 mg sodium; 0 mg cholesterol

Smoothies

Although I've included smoothies in the breakfast section, they also make wonderful desserts. The secret to making a good smoothie is using frozen fruit, which makes it really thick and cold. Try the following smoothies for starters, then begin experimenting with your own combinations.

Strawberry Smoothie

Serves 2

Try this cold, thick smoothie with whole grain cereal or muffins for a delicious and satisfying breakfast. You can buy frozen strawberries or freeze your own in an airtight container. To freeze bananas, peel them and break into inch-long pieces. Pack loosely in an airtight container and freeze. Bananas will keep in the freezer for about two months, strawberries for six months.

1   **cup frozen strawberries**
1   **cup frozen banana chunks**
1/2-1 **cup unsweetened apple juice**

Place all the ingredients into a blender and process on high speed until smooth. You may have to stop the blender occasionally and move the unblended fruit to the center with a spatula in order to get the smoothie smooth!

Per serving: 97 calories (0% from fat)
           1 g protein; 22 g carbohydrate; 0 g fat; 5 mg sodium; 0 mg cholesterol

Peach Smoothie

Serves 1

This smoothie is such a treat! It reminds me of fresh peach ice cream. You can freeze your own peaches when they are in season, or purchase frozen peaches at your supermarket.

1   **peach, sliced and frozen**
3/4-1 **cup vanilla soy milk or rice milk**
1   **teaspoon sugar or other sweetener**

Combine all ingredients in a blender and process until smooth. Serve immediately.

Per serving: 156 calories (9% from fat)
                    4 g protein; 29 g carbohydrate; 1 g fat; 68 mg sodium; 0 mg cholesterol

Apricot Smoothie

Serves 2

This is an absolutely delicious smoothie. To freeze fresh apricots, cut or break them in half and remove the pits, then layer them loosely in airtight containers or freezer bags. They will keep for six months to a year. You can also drain and freeze water-packed canned apricots for this smoothie. To freeze bananas, peel them, then cut or break into 1-inch pieces. Pack loosely in airtight containers or freezer bags.

1   **cup frozen banana pieces**
1   **cup frozen apricot halves**
1/4   **cup undiluted apple juice concentrate**
3/4   **cup soy milk or rice milk**

Combine all the ingredients in a blender and process until smooth. Serve immediately.

Per serving: 181 calories (6% from fat)
                    3 g protein; 40 g carbohydrate; 1 g fat; 44 mg sodium; 0 mg cholesterol

BREADS & MUFFINS

Pumpkin Spice Muffins

Makes 10 to 12 muffins

2   **cups whole wheat or whole wheat pastry flour**
1/2   **cup sugar**
1   **tablespoon baking powder**
1/2   **teaspoon baking soda**
1/2   **teaspoon salt**
1/2   **teaspoon cinnamon**
1/4   **teaspoon nutmeg**

1   **15-ounce can solid-pack pumpkin**
1/2   **cup water**
1/2   **cup raisins**

Preheat the oven to 375°F.   Mix the flour, sugar, baking powder, baking soda, salt, cinnamon, and nutmeg in a large bowl.   Add the pumpkin, water, and raisins, and stir until just mixed.

Lightly oil-spray muffin cups and fill to the top. Bake 25 to 30 minutes, until the tops of the muffins bounce back when pressed lightly. Let stand 1 to 2 minutes, before removing from the pan. When cool, store in an airtight container in the refrigerator.

Per muffin: 137 calories (0% from fat);
              3 g protein; 31 g carbohydrate; 0 g fat; 128 mg sodium; 0 mg cholesterol

Double Whammy Brannies

Makes 12 muffins

These wholesome, fruity muffins contain two types of bran. Prune puree makes them moist without added fat. Look for it under the names WonderSlim or Lekvar, or use a 4-ounce jar of prune baby food. The muffins will be quite moist when they first come out of the oven, so let them stand a few minutes before serving.

2	**cups whole wheat or whole wheat pastry flour**
3/4	**cup wheat bran**
3/4	**cup oat bran**
1/2	**teaspoon salt**
1	**teaspoon baking soda**
1	**teaspoon cinnamon**
1/4	**teaspoon nutmeg**
1	**apple, finely chopped or grated (use a food processor)**
1/2	**cup raisins**
11/2	**cups soy milk or rice milk**
11/2	**tablespoons vinegar**
1/4	**cup prune puree, WonderSlim, or prune baby food**
1/3	**cup molasses**

Preheat the oven to 350°F. Mix the flour, brans, salt, soda and spices. In a separate bowl mix the remaining ingredients. Combine the wet and dry ingredients and stir to mix.

Spoon into muffin pans which have been sprayed with a nonstick spray and bake until the tops bounce back when lightly pressed, about 25 minutes. Let stand 1 to 2 minutes, then remove from pan and let stand an additional 5 minutes before serving.

Per muffin: 171 calories (5% from fat)
5 g protein; 35 g carbohydrate; 1 g fat; 199 mg sodium; 0 mg cholesterol

Quick and Easy Brown Bread

Makes 1 loaf (about 20 slices)

This bread is similar to Boston Brown Bread, sweet and moist with no added fat or oil. It is quick to mix and requires no kneading or rising. It is especially delicious with orange marmalade.

11/2	**cups soy milk**
2	**tablespoons vinegar**
2	**cups whole wheat flour**
1	**cup unbleached flour**
2	**teaspoons baking soda**
1/2	**teaspoon salt**
1/2	**cup molasses**
1/2	**cup raisins**

orange marmalade for serving (optional)

Preheat the oven to 325°F. Mix the soy milk with vinegar and set aside.

In a large bowl stir the whole wheat flour, unbleached flour, soda and salt together. Add the soy milk mixture and molasses. Stir to mix, then stir in the raisins. Do not overmix. Spoon into a large nonstick or oil-sprayed loaf pan and bake for one hour.

Per slice: 111 calories (0% from fat);
            3 g protein; 24 g carbohydrate; 0 g fat; 149 mg sodium; 0 mg cholesterol

Cornbread

Serves 9

Leaving the oil out makes this cornbread slightly moister than its higher fat counterpart. Serve it with Quick Chili Beans (page 117) or any other soup or stew.

11/2 **cups soy milk**
11/2 **tablespoons vinegar**

1   **cup cornmeal**
1   **cup unbleached flour**
2   **tablespoons sugar or other sweetener**
1   **teaspoon baking powder**
1/2 **teaspoon baking soda**
1/2 **teaspoon salt**

Preheat the oven to 425° F. Combine the soy milk and vinegar and set aside.

Mix the cornmeal, unbleached flour, sugar, baking powder, baking soda, and salt in a large bowl. Add the soy milk mixture and stir until just mixed. Spread the batter evenly in an oil-sprayed 9 x 9-inch baking dish. Bake until the top is golden brown, 25 to 30 minutes. Serve hot.

Per serving: 124 calories (4% from fat)
                3 g protein; 26 g carbohydrate; 1 g fat; 180 mg sodium; 0 mg cholesterol

Garlic Bread

Makes about 20 slices

*Roasted garlic makes a delicious, fat-free garlic bread. Choose heads with
nice big cloves for easy peeling.*

2   heads of garlic

1-2   teaspoons mixed Italian herbs
1/2   teaspoon salt
1   baguette or loaf of French bread, sliced

Roast the whole, unpeeled garlic heads in a 400°F oven (or toaster oven)
for about 30 minutes, until they feel soft when gently squeezed.

Peel the cloves, or squeeze them out of their skin, and place them in a
bowl. Mash them into a paste with a fork, then mix in the herbs and
salt. Spread onto the sliced bread. Wrap tightly in foil and bake at
350°F for 20 minutes.

Per slice: 68 calories (0% from fat)
            2 g protein; 12 g carbohydrate; 0 g fat; 154 mg sodium; 0 mg cholesterol

Crostini with Roasted Red Peppers

Makes about 20 slices

In this fat-free version of crostini, thin slices of toasted bread are topped with a flavorful blend of tomatoes and roasted red peppers. You'll find sun-dried tomatoes in the dried fruit section of many markets. Roasted red peppers packed in water are usually found near the pickles and olives.

1	**cup boiling water**
10	**sun-dried tomato halves**
2/3	**cup roasted red peppers (about 2 peppers)**
1	**garlic clove, crushed**
2	**tablespoons fresh basil, finely chopped — OR —**
	1 teaspoon dried basil
1/8	**teaspoon black pepper**
1	**small baguette, cut into 1/2-inch thick slices**

Pour the boiling water over the tomatoes and set aside until softened, about 30 minutes.

Drain the tomatoes and coarsely chop them. Chop the roasted red peppers and add to the tomatoes, along with the garlic, basil, and pepper. Let stand 30 minutes.

Preheat the oven to 350°F. Slice the baguette and arrange the slices in a single layer on a baking sheet. Toast in the preheated oven until the outsides are crisp, 10 to 15 minutes. Remove from the oven and cool slightly, then spread each piece with some of the tomato mixture.

Per slice: 93 calories (0% from fat)
3 g protein; 18 g carbohydrate; 0 g fat ; 179 mg sodium; 0 mg cholesterol

SANDWICHES, SAUCES, & SPREADS

Garbanzo Salad Sandwich

Makes 4 sandwiches

Garbanzo beans make a delicious sandwich spread.

1	cup cooked garbanzo beans, drained
1	celery stalk, finely sliced
1	green onion, finely chopped, including green top
1	tablespoon Fat-Free Nayonaise (optional)
2	teaspoons stoneground mustard
2	tablespoons sweet pickle relish
1/4	teaspoon salt (optional)
8	slices whole wheat bread or 4 pieces of pita bread
4	lettuce leaves
4	tomato slices

Mash the garbanzo beans with a fork or potato masher, leaving some chunks. Add the celery, green onion, Nayonaise (if using), mustard, and relish. Add salt to taste.

Spread on whole wheat bread or serve in pita bread with lettuce and sliced tomatoes.

Per sandwich: 182 calories (14% from fat)
           7 g protein; 32 g carbohydrate; 3 g fat; 337 mg sodium; 0 mg cholesterol

Missing Egg Salad

Makes about 1 cup (enough for 4 sandwiches)

Serve as a dip with fresh vegetables or pita wedges, or as a sandwich spread on fresh whole grain bread.

    1   **cup firm tofu (1/2 pound), mashed**
    1   **green onion, finely chopped, including green top**
    2   **tablespoons pickle relish**
    2   **tablespoons Fat-Free Nayonaise (optional)**
    2   **teaspoons stoneground mustard**
    2   **teaspoons soy sauce**
    1/4 **teaspoon each: cumin, turmeric, and garlic powder**

Combine all ingredients. Check and adjust seasonings if necessary.

Per sandwich: 188 calories (17% from fat)
              10 g protein; 28 g carbohydrate; 4 g fat; 246 mg sodium; 0 mg cholesterol

Black Bean Sauce

Makes 2 cups

Serve this creamy black bean sauce over broccoli, potatoes, or pasta.

    1   **15-ounce can black beans, drained**
    1/4 **cup roasted red pepper**
    2   **tablespoons lemon juice**
    1/2 **teaspoon each: chili powder and garlic granules or powder**
    1/4 **teaspoon each: cumin and coriander**
    1/4 **cup chopped fresh cilantro (optional)**

Puree all ingredients in a food processor or blender until very smooth.

Per 1/4-cup: 72 calories (0% from fat)
              4 g protein; 13 g carbohydrate; 0 g fat; 73 mg of sodium; 0 mg cholesterol

Hummus (Chickpea Paté)

Makes about 2 cups

This Middle Eastern paté can be used as a sandwich spread or as a dip with crackers, wedges of pita bread or fresh vegetable slices. It is easily prepared with a food processor.

2	**garlic cloves**
1	**tablespoon fresh parsley**
1	**15-ounce can garbanzo beans**
2	**tablespoons lemon juice**
1/4	**teaspoon salt**
1/4	**teaspoon cumin**
1/4	**teaspoon paprika**

Chop the garlic and parsley in a food processor, scraping down sides of bowl to make sure everything is finely chopped.

Drain the garbanzo beans, reserving the liquid. Add the beans to the food processor, along with the lemon juice, salt, cumin, and paprika. Process until smooth and spreadable, adding about 1/2 cup of the reserved bean liquid to achieve a spreadable consistency.

Per 1/4 cup: 70 calories (10% from fat)
          3 g protein; 12 g carbohydrate; 1 g fat; 203 mg sodium; 0 mg cholesterol

Creamy Cucumber Dip
Serves 6

Serve this cool, creamy dip with wedges of fresh pita bread.

1	**medium cucumber**
1/2	**pound firm tofu**
2	**tablespoons lemon juice**
1	**garlic clove, peeled**
1/4	**teaspoon salt**
1/8	**teaspoon each: cumin and coriander**
	pinch cayenne
2	**tablespoons minced red onion**

Peel, seed, and grate the cucumber. Let stand 10 minutes.

In a food processor, combine the tofu, lemon juice, garlic, salt, cumin, coriander, and cayenne. Blend until completely smooth.

Squeeze the cucumbers to remove any liquid then mix them with the red onion and tofu mixture. Chill 1 to 2 hours before serving.

Per 1/4-cup: 44 calories (21% from fat)
4 g protein; 4 g carbohydrate; 1 g fat; 92 mg of sodium; 0 mg cholesterol

Almost Instant Bean Dip
Makes about 2 cups

Instant bean flakes (black or pinto) make a quick dip or filling for burritos. They are sold in natural food stores and some supermarkets. My favorite brands are "Fantastic Foods" and "Taste Adventure."

1	**cup instant bean flakes**
1	**cup boiling water**
1/2-1	**cup salsa (you choose the heat)**
	baked tortilla chips for serving

Mix the bean flakes and boiling water. Let stand 5 minutes, then stir in salsa to taste. Serve with baked tortilla chips.

Per 1/4 cup: 49 calories (0% from fat)
3 g protein; 9 g carbohydrate; 0 g fat; 150 mg sodium; 0 mg cholesterol

SALADS & DRESSINGS

Spinach Salad with Curry Dressing

Serves 6 to 8

*This wonderful spinach salad is a happy marriage of flavors and textures.
It is especially easy to make when you use the prewashed fresh spinach,
available in the produce department of most markets.*

1   **bunch fresh spinach, washed or** 1/2 **bag prewashed spinach**
1   **green apple, diced**
2   **green onions, finely sliced, including green tops**
1/4 **cup golden raisins**

3   **tablespoons seasoned rice vinegar**
3   **tablespoons frozen apple juice concentrate**
2   **teaspoons stoneground mustard**
1   **teaspoon soy sauce**
1/2 **teaspoon curry powder**
1/4 **teaspoon black pepper**

Combine the washed spinach with the apple, onions, and raisins.

Combine the vinegar, apple juice concentrate, mustard, soy sauce, curry
powder, and black pepper in a small bowl and whisk together. Pour over
salad and toss to mix just before serving.

Per serving: 45 calories (0% from fat)
              1 g protein; 9 g carbohydrate; 0 g fat; 210 mg sodium; 0 mg cholesterol

Crispy Green Salad

Serves 6

This cool, crisp salad is a welcome addition to any meal.

4	cups torn or chopped romaine lettuce
1	cup finely shredded green or red cabbage
1	cup thinly sliced celery
1	15-ounce can garbanzo beans
1/4	cup thinly sliced red onion
2	tablespoons seasoned rice vinegar
1	tablespoon apple cider vinegar
1/2	teaspoon sugar or other sweetener
1/4	teaspoon dried basil
1/4	teaspoon mixed Italian herbs
1/4	teaspoon garlic granules or powder
1/8	teaspoon salt
1/8	teaspoon black pepper

Combine the lettuce, cabbage, and celery in a salad bowl. Drain the garbanzo beans, reserving the liquid, and add them to the salad along with the sliced red onion.

In a small bowl, stir together the vinegars, sugar, basil, Italian herbs, garlic granules, salt, and pepper. Stir in 2 tablespoons of the reserved bean liquid. Just before serving, pour the dressing over the salad and toss to mix.

Per serving: 106 calories (5% from fat)
4 g protein; 21 g carbohydrate; 1 g fat; 334 mg sodium; 0 mg cholesterol

Mixed Greens with Quick Piquant Dressing

Serves 6

Prewashed salad greens are available in most supermarkets and natural food stores. These mixes are colorful and flavorful, and stand well on their own, with just a touch of dressing. Other vegetables can be added for additional flavor and nutrition, as in the following recipe.

1/2	**red or yellow bell pepper, seeded and sliced**
1	**red or yellow tomato, sliced**
1	**cup sliced or diced jicama**
6	**cups prewashed salad mix**
3	**tablespoons seasoned rice vinegar**
3	**tablespoons of your favorite salsa**

Combine the pepper, tomato, jicama, and salad mix in a large bowl.

Mix the seasoned rice vinegar and salsa and pour over the salad. Toss gently to mix.

Per serving: 28 calories (0% from fat)
              1 g protein; 5 g carbohydrate; 0 g fat; 160 mg sodium; 0 mg cholesterol

Ensalada de Frijoles

Serves 4 as a complete meal

This salad has it all: rice, beans, corn, and greens. It is quick to prepare, especially if you use prewashed salad mix, and makes a perfect meal on a hot day. Jicama (pronounced "hick-ama")is a delicious root vegetable that is delightfully crisp and slightly sweet. It is usually sold in the unrefrigerated area of your supermarket's produce section.

- **3   cups (approximately) cooked brown rice, (page 97)**

- **8   cups prewashed salad mix**
- **2   carrots, grated or cut into small julienne strips**
- **1   15-ounce can black beans, drained and rinsed**
- **1   cup peeled and grated jicama**
- **2   tomatoes, diced or cut into wedges**
- **1   15-ounce can corn, drained (or 2 cups fresh or frozen)**
- **1/2   cup cilantro leaves, coarsely chopped (optional)**

- **1/4   cup of your favorite salsa**
- **1/4   cup seasoned rice vinegar**
- **1   garlic clove, crushed or pressed**

additional salsa for topping

Make a bed of warm brown rice on each of four plates. Top each with layers of salad mix, carrot, black beans, jicama, tomatoes, corn, and cilantro leaves.

Mix the salsa, seasoned rice vinegar, and crushed garlic. Sprinkle over each of the salads, then top with generous spoonfuls of salsa.

Per serving: 302 calories (5% from fat)
              10 g protein; 60 g carbohydrate; 2 g fat; 355 mg sodium; 0 mg cholesterol

Variation: Substitute warmed corn tortillas (about 2 per plate) for the brown rice.

Variation: Good Seasons Fat-Free Italian Dressing is a nice alternative dressing on this salad. I like to mix it with a bit of salsa before adding it to the salad.

Aztec Salad

Serves 10

This salad is a celebration of flavor and color. It may be made in advance, and keeps well for several days. If you dislike cilantro, simply omit it from the recipe.

2   **15-ounce cans black beans, drained and rinsed**
1/2 **cup finely chopped red onion**
1   **green bell pepper, seeded and diced**
1   **red or yellow bell pepper, seeded and diced**
2   **cups corn kernels, canned, frozen, or fresh**
2   **tomatoes, diced**
3/4 **cup chopped fresh cilantro (optional)**

2   **tablespoons seasoned rice vinegar**
2   **tablespoons apple cider or distilled vinegar**
2   **garlic cloves, pressed or finely minced**
1   **lemon or lime, juiced**
2   **teaspoons ground cumin**
1   **teaspoon coriander**
1/2 **teaspoon crushed red pepper or a pinch of cayenne**

In a large bowl, combine the rinsed beans with the red onion, bell peppers, corn, tomatoes, and cilantro.

Whisk together the vinegars with the garlic, lemon or lime juice, cumin, coriander, and red pepper flakes. Pour over the salad and toss gently to mix.

Per serving: 143 calories (0% from fat)
              7 g protein; 30 g carbohydrate; 0 g fat; 171 mg sodium; 0 mg cholesterol

Three Bean Salad

Serves 8

This salad is delicious all by itself or as an addition to a green salad. I like to mix it with torn romaine lettuce leaves for a quick, nearly-instant salad.

1	15-ounce can kidney beans, drained
1	15-ounce can garbanzo beans, drained
1	15-ounce can green beans, drained
1/2	small red onion, finely chopped
1/4	cup finely chopped fresh parsley
1/2	cup cider vinegar
2	tablespoons seasoned rice vinegar
3	garlic cloves, minced
1/2	teaspoon basil
1/4	teaspoon oregano
1/4	teaspoon marjoram
1/4	teaspoon black pepper

Drain the beans and place them in large bowl with the chopped onion and parsley.

In a separate bowl whisk the vinegars, garlic, and seasonings together. Add to the beans and toss to mix. If possible, refrigerate for 2 to 3 hours before serving.

Per serving: 141 calories (6% from fat)
7 g protein; 26 g carbohydrate; 1 g fat; 140 mg sodium; 0 mg cholesterol

Four Bean Salad

Serves 10

This colorful salad is quick to prepare and keeps well.

1	15-ounce can dark kidney beans, drained
1	15-ounce can black-eyed peas, drained
1	10-ounce package frozen lima beans, thawed
1	15-ounce can vegetarian chili beans (do not drain)
1	large red bell pepper, diced
1/2	cup finely chopped onion
2	cups corn, canned, frozen, or fresh
1/4	cup seasoned rice vinegar
2	tablespoons apple cider or distilled vinegar
1	lemon, juiced
2	teaspoons cumin
1	teaspoon coriander
1/8	teaspoon cayenne

Drain the kidney beans and black-eyed peas and place them in a large bowl. Add the lima beans, and the chili beans with their sauce. Stir in the bell pepper, onion, and corn.

Whisk the vinegars, lemon juice and seasonings together and pour over the salad. Toss gently to mix. Chill at least 1 hour before serving, if possible.

Per serving: 216 calories (0% from fat)
            11 g protein; 41 g carbohydrate; 0 g fat; 104 mg sodium; 0 mg cholesterol

White Bean Salad

Serves 4 to 6

You'll love the tangy flavor of this super-easy salad.

1	**15-ounce can white beans, drained and rinsed**
1	**small red bell pepper, diced**
1/2	**cup finely chopped fresh parsley**
1	**lemon, juiced (2-3 tablespoons)**
2	**teaspoons balsamic vinegar**
1/4	**teaspoon garlic granules or powder**
1/4	**teaspoon black pepper**

Combine all ingredients in a large bowl. Let stand 10 to 15 minutes before serving.

Per serving: 103 calories 0% from fat)
6 g protein; 19 g carbohydrate; 0 g fat; 184 mg sodium; 0 mg cholesterol

Pasta Salad

Serves 8

This salad is delicious hot or cold. Use fat-free Italian dressing, available in most markets or the Fat-Free Vinaigrette on page 64.

8	ounces uncooked pasta (spirals, shells, etc.)
10	sun-dried tomato halves
1	cup cooked kidney beans, drained
1	cup cooked garbanzo beans, drained
1	red bell pepper, seeded and diced
4	green onions, sliced
1	15-ounce can water-packed artichoke hearts, drained and quartered
1	cup fat-free Italian dressing

Cook the pasta in boiling water until it is just tender. Rinse and drain, then place it into a large bowl.

Soak the sun-dried tomatoes in about 1 cup of boiling water until they are soft, then chop them and add to the pasta, along with all the remaining ingredients. Toss gently to mix.

Per serving: 198 calories (3% from fat)
7 g protein; 40 g carbohydrate; 1 g fat; 157 mg sodium; 0 mg cholesterol

Tip: Good Seasons makes a fat-free Italian Dressing mix that is very good and goes well with this salad.

Red Potato Salad

Serves 8

Red potatoes make a beautiful and delicious salad.

4	**large red potatoes, scrubbed**
1/2	**cup thinly sliced red onion**
1	**red or yellow bell pepper, seeded and sliced**
1/4	**cup finely chopped fresh parsley**
1/4	**cup cider vinegar**
1/4	**cup lemon juice**
2	**tablespoons seasoned rice vinegar**
2	**garlic cloves, crushed**
2	**teaspoons stoneground mustard**
1/2	**teaspoon salt**
1/4-1/2	**teaspoon black pepper**

Cut the potatoes into 1/2-inch cubes and steam over boiling water until just tender, 10 to 15 minutes. As soon as the potatoes are tender, rinse them with cold water and place them in a large bowl. Add the red onion, bell pepper, and parsley.

Mix the remaining ingredients and pour over the potatoes. Toss gently to mix.

Per serving: 128 calories (0% from fat)
2 g protein; 29 g carbohydrate; 0 g fat; 233 mg of sodium; 0 mg cholesterol

Old-Fashioned Potato Salad

Serves 8

The creamy dressing on this salad is made with fat-free Nayonaise or silken tofu. Both are sold in natural food stores and many supermarkets.

4	**medium russet potatoes (about 6 cups diced)**
2	**celery stalks, including leaves, thinly sliced**
1/2	**cup finely chopped red onion**
1/2	**cup finely chopped parsley**
1/2	**cup finely shredded green cabbage (optional)**
1/2	**cup Fat-Free Nayonaise — OR —** 1/2 **cup silken tofu**
2	**tablespoons seasoned rice vinegar**
2	**tablespoons cider vinegar**
1	**tablespoon stoneground mustard**
1/2	**teaspoon dill weed**
1/4	**teaspoon turmeric**
1/4	**teaspoon celery seeds**
1/4	**teaspoon salt**
1/4	**teaspoon black pepper**

Scrub the potatoes, peel them if you wish, and cut them into 1/2-inch cubes. Steam over boiling water until just tender, about 15 minutes, then transfer to a large bowl. Add the celery, onion, parsley, and cabbage.

Combine all the remaining ingredients, and blend until totally smooth, (use a food processor to do this if using silken tofu). Pour over the salad. Toss gently to mix. Chill if time allows.

Per serving: 130 calories (0% from fat)
   2 g protein; 30 g carbohydrate; 0 g fat; 340 mg sodium; 0 mg cholesterol

Tip: Potatoes will soak up the dressing as the salad sits, so if it seems dry after it's been stored, add a tablespoon or two of water to restore a moist, creamy texture.

Cucumbers with Creamy Dill Dressing

Serves 6

The dressing for this cool, creamy salad is made with silken tofu which is sold in most supermarkets under the brand name "Mori-Nu." Using the lite variety, if you can find it, will further reduce the fat.

1	**10.5-ounce package firm silken tofu**
11/2	**teaspoons garlic granules or powder**
1/2	**teaspoon dill weed**
1/2	**teaspoon salt**
11/2	**tablespoons lemon juice**
1	**tablespoon seasoned rice vinegar**
2	**cucumbers, peeled and thinly sliced**
1/2	**cup thinly sliced red onion**

Blend the tofu, garlic granules, dill weed, salt, 2 tablespoons of water, lemon juice, and seasoned rice vinegar in a food processor or blender until completely smooth.

Place the cucumbers and sliced red onion into a salad bowl. Add the dressing and toss to mix. Chill before serving.

Per serving: 64 calories (14% from fat)
              6 g protein; 7 g carbohydrate; 1 g fat; 232 mg sodium; 0 mg cholesterol

Cucumber and Tomato Salad

Serves 6

This salad is colorful and quick to make. Serve it as a cool contrast with chili, curries, and other spicy foods.

3   **cucumbers**
2   **tomatoes, diced**
1/2   **small red onion, thinly sliced**
1/2   **teaspoon basil**
1/2   **teaspoon dill weed**
1   **tablespoon chopped fresh parsley**
balsamic or apple cider vinegar

Peel the cucumbers, slice them in half lengthwise, and scoop out the seeds. Cut the cucumbers into bite-sized pieces and place in a bowl. Add the tomatoes and red onion, then sprinkle with basil, dill, and fresh parsley. Add enough vinegar to coat all the vegetables, and toss to mix. Chill before serving if possible.

Per serving: 35 calories (0% from fat)
             1 g protein; 7 g carbohydrate; 0 g fat; 7 mg sodium; 0 mg cholesterol

Rootin' Tootin' Salad

Serves 6

Three root vegetables, beets, jicama, and carrots, combine to make a crunchy, nutritious salad.

2-3	**medium beets**
1	**small jicama, peeled and cut in thin strips or diced**
2	**carrots, peeled and cut in thin strips or diced**
3	**tablespoons lemon juice**
2	**tablespoons seasoned rice vinegar**
2	**teaspoons stoneground mustard**
1/2	**teaspoon dill weed**

Cut the stems and roots off the beets, then steam them until they are tender, about 20 minutes. When they are cool enough to handle, slip the skins off and cut the beets into slices or cubes. Place them into a salad bowl, along with the jicama and carrots. Mix the lemon juice, vinegar, mustard, and dill, and pour over the salad. Toss to mix.

Per serving: 35 calories (0% from fat)
1 g protein; 7 g carbohydrate; 0 g fat; 147 mg sodium; 0 mg cholesterol

Desi's Carrot Coins

Serves 2

Desi, my 9-year old neighbor, taught me how delicious fresh vegetables are with just a bit of lemon (or lime) juice and salt. These are great for snacking , or you can add them to other salads.

2	**carrots**
1/2	**lemon or lime, juiced (about 2 tablespoons)**
1/4	**teaspoon salt**

Cut the carrots into 1/4-inch thick rounds (coins) and place them in a bowl. Sprinkle with lemon or lime juice and salt. Let stand 20 minutes before serving.

Per serving: 35 calories (0% from fat)
1 g protein; 8 g carbohydrate; 0 g fat; 291 mg sodium; 0 mg cholesterol

Fat-Free Vinaigrette

Makes 1/2 cup

This is a perfect everyday dressing. Based on seasoned rice vinegar, it has no fat and is simple to prepare. You can keep it in the refrigerator for 2 to 3 weeks.

1/2   **cup seasoned rice vinegar**
1-2   **teaspoons stoneground mustard**
1   **garlic clove, crushed or pressed**

Whisk all ingredients together. Use as a dressing for salads and for steamed vegetables.

Per tablespoon: 6 calories (0% from fat)
            0 g protein; 2 g carbohydrate; 0 g fat; 310 mg sodium; 0 mg cholesterol

Balsamic Vinaigrette

Makes 1/3 cup

Balsamic vinegar is a flavorful Italian wine vinegar available in most markets.

2   **tablespoons balsamic vinegar**
2   **tablespoons seasoned rice vinegar**
2   **tablespoons water**
1-2   **garlic cloves, crushed or pressed**

Whisk all ingredients together.

Per tablespoon: 6 calories (0% from fat)
            0 g protein; 2 g carbohydrate; 0 g fat; 99 mg sodium; 0 mg cholesterol

Curry Dressing

Makes 1/2 cup

3	tablespoons seasoned rice vinegar
3	tablespoons water
2	teaspoons stoneground mustard
1	teaspoon soy sauce
1	teaspoon sugar or other sweetener
1/2	teaspoon curry powder
1/4	teaspoon black pepper

Whisk all ingredients together.

Per tablespoon: 9 calories (0% from fat)
        0 g protein; 2 g carbohydrate; 0 g fat; 151 mg sodium; 0 mg cholesterol

Raspberry Vinaigrette

Makes 1/3 cup

Raspberry vinegar has a mild fruity taste, well-suited to salad dressing.

2	tablespoons raspberry vinegar
2	tablespoons seasoned rice vinegar
2	tablespoons water
1/4	teaspoon crushed rosemary
1/4	teaspoon tarragon

Whisk all ingredients together.

Per tablespoon: 5 calories (0% from fat)
        0 g protein; 1 g carbohydrate; 0 g fat; 74 mg sodium; 0 mg cholesterol

Creamy Dill Dressing

Makes about 1 1/2 cups

This creamy dressing has no added oil. It is made with silken tofu which is available in most markets. Mori Nu is one widely distributed brand.

1	**10.5-ounce package firm silken tofu**
1 1/2	**teaspoons garlic granules or powder**
1/2	**teaspoon dill weed**
1/2	**teaspoon salt**
2	**tablespoons water**
1 1/2	**tablespoons lemon juice**
1	**tablespoon seasoned rice vinegar**

Combine all the ingredients in a food processor or blender and blend until completely smooth. Refrigerate extra dressing in an airtight container.

Per tablespoon: 23 calories (20% from fat)
3 g protein; 2 g carbohydrate; 0.5 g fat; 115 mg sodium; 0 mg cholesterol

Piquant Dressing

Makes about 1/3 cup

1/4	**cup seasoned rice vinegar**
2	**tablespoons ketchup**
1	**teaspoon stone ground mustard**
1	**garlic clove, pressed or crushed**
1/2	**teaspoon paprika**
1/4	**teaspoon oregano**
1/8	**teaspoon ground cumin**

Whisk all ingredients together.

Per tablespoon: 12 calories (0% from fat)
0 g protein; 2 g carbohydrate; 0 g fat; 210 mg sodium; 0 mg cholesterol

SOUPS & STEWS

Curried Lentil Soup

Serves 8

When instant soup cups first came on the market, I fell in love with Curried Lentil Soup. This is my homemade version. Serve it with cooked greens (page 85) and fresh bread or chapatis.

1	cup lentils, rinsed
1	onion, chopped
2	celery stalks, sliced
4	garlic cloves, minced
1	teaspoon whole cumin seed
8	cups water or vegetable stock
1/2	cup uncooked couscous
1	cup crushed tomatoes
1 1/2	teaspoons curry powder
1/8	teaspoon black pepper
1	teaspoon salt

Place the lentils, onion, celery, garlic, cumin seed, and water or vegetable stock in a large pot. Bring to a simmer then cover loosely and cook until the lentils are tender, about 50 minutes.

Stir in couscous, crushed tomatoes, curry powder, and pepper. Continue cooking until couscous is tender, about 10 minutes. Add salt to taste.

Per serving: 111 calories (0% from fat)
6 g protein; 21 g carbohydrate; 0 g fat; 327 mg of sodium; 0 mg cholesterol

Green Velvet Soup

Serves 10

This beautiful soup is a delicious way of eating green vegetables.

1   **onion, chopped**
2   **celery stalks, sliced**
2   **potatoes, scrubbed and diced**
3/4 **cup split peas, rinsed**
2   **bay leaves**
6   **cups water or vegetable stock**

2   **medium zucchini, diced**
1   **medium stalk broccoli, chopped**
1   **bunch fresh spinach, washed and chopped**
1/2 **teaspoon basil**
1/4 **teaspoon black pepper**
1   **teaspoon salt**

Place the onion, celery, potatoes, split peas, and bay leaves in a large pot with water or stock and bring to a boil. Lower the heat, cover, and simmer 1 hour. Remove the bay leaves.

Add the zucchini, broccoli, spinach, basil, and black pepper. Simmer 20 minutes. Transfer to a blender in several small batches and blend until completely smooth, holding the lid on tightly. Return to the pot and heat until steamy. Add salt to taste.

Per serving: 120 calories (0% from fat)
            5 g protein; 24 g carbohydrate; 0 g fat; 238 mg sodium; 0 mg cholesterol

Tomato Soup

Serves 6 to 8

Tomato Soup is one of my comfort foods, perfect for cold, rainy days. This version is made with canned tomatoes and is quick and easy to prepare. Serve it with bread or muffins. For a heartier soup, add some cooked brown rice.

1	small onion, chopped
3	celery stalks, sliced
1	28-ounce can crushed or ground tomatoes
2 1/2	teaspoons sugar or other sweetener
1/2	teaspoon paprika
1/2	teaspoon basil
1/4	teaspoon pepper
3	cups soy milk
1/2	teaspoon salt

Combine the onion, celery, tomatoes, sugar, paprika, basil, and pepper in a pot. Cover and simmer 15 minutes, stirring occasionally.

Transfer to a blender in small batches and process until very smooth, adding some of the soy milk to each batch. Start the blender on low speed and hold the lid on tightly. Put the soup through a sieve if a perfectly smooth soup is desired. Add salt to taste, then return the soup to its pot and heat it over a low flame until it is steamy.

Per serving: 80 calories (10% from fat)
3 g protein; 16 g carbohydrate; 1 g fat; 442 mg sodium; 0 mg cholesterol

Minestrone

Serves 8

This tomato-vegetable soup is delicious as is, or enhance it with additional vegetables of your choosing. Add fresh-baked bread or muffins and a salad for a satisfying meal.

1	small onion, chopped
4	garlic cloves, minced
2	carrots, cut into chunks
2	celery stalks, sliced including tops
2	medium potatoes, scrubbed and cut into chunks
2	tablespoons chopped parsley
4	cups tomato juice
4	cups water or vegetable stock
1	teaspoon mixed Italian herbs
1/4	teaspoon black pepper
1	medium zucchini, diced
1/2	cup pasta shells
1	15-ounce can kidney beans, drained
1-2	cups finely chopped kale, collard greens, or spinach
2	tablespoons chopped fresh basil or 2 teaspoons dried basil

Place the onion, garlic, carrots, celery, potatoes, and parsley in a large pot with the tomato juice, water or stock, Italian herbs, and black pepper. Bring to a simmer, then cover and cook 20 minutes.

Add the zucchini, pasta, kidney beans, chopped greens, and basil. Cover and simmer until the pasta is tender, about 20 minutes. Add extra tomato juice or water if the soup seems too thick.

Per serving: 158 calories (0% from fat)
6 g protein; 33 g carbohydrate; 0 g fat; 347 mg sodium; 0 mg cholesterol

Creamy Lima Soup

Serves 4 to 6

This soup is quick and delicious. Use fresh basil and parsley if possible. They really make the soup.

1	**onion, chopped**
1	**large garlic clove, minced**
1	**cup crushed tomatoes**
2	**cups shredded green cabbage**
2	**tablespoons fresh basil or 1 teaspoon dried basil**
1	**15-ounce can lima beans, drained**
1	**15-ounce can Swanson's Vegetable Broth**
1	**cup soy milk**
2	**tablespoons chopped fresh parsley**
1/2	**teaspoon salt**
1/8	**teaspoon black pepper**

Heat 1/2 cup of water in a large pot then add the onion and garlic and cook until the onion is soft, about 5 minutes. Add the tomatoes, cabbage, basil, lima beans, and the vegetable broth. Simmer for 15 minutes.

Ladle about 3 cups of the soup into a blender and add the soy milk, parsley, salt, and pepper. Blend until smooth, using a low speed and holding the lid on tightly. Return it to the pot and heat gently (do not boil) until very hot and steamy.

Per serving: 145 calories (5% from fat)
              6 g protein; 28 g carbohydrate; 1 g fat; 308 mg sodium; 0 mg cholesterol

Potato and Cabbage Soup

Serves 6 to 8

4   potatoes, peeled and diced
1   large onion, chopped
4   cups shredded green cabbage
4   cups water or vegetable stock

1   cup soy milk or rice milk
1/4   teaspoon black pepper
1/2-1 teaspoon salt

Place the potatoes, onion, and cabbage in a large pot with the water or vegetable stock. Bring to a simmer and cook 15 minutes.

Remove about 3 cups of the soup to a blender and add the soy milk or rice milk. Blend until smooth then return it to the pot and stir to mix. Add pepper and salt to taste.

Per serving: 139 calories (0% from fat)
                    3 g protein; 31 g carbohydrate; 0 g fat; 292 mg sodium; 0 mg cholesterol

Black Bean Soup

Serves 6

This is a great soup to make ahead, because it actually tastes better the second day.

1	onion, chopped
3	garlic cloves, crushed
2	celery stalks, sliced
1	carrot, diced
1	potato, diced
2	cups vegetable stock or water
2	15-ounce cans black beans, undrained
1	teaspoon oregano
1	teaspoon cumin
1	tablespoon lemon juice

fresh cilantro for garnish (optional)

Place all of the ingredients except the lemon juice and cilantro into a large pot and bring to a simmer. Cover and cook 15 minutes.

Pour about 3 cups of the soup into a blender and blend on low speed until smooth. Be sure to hold the lid on tightly. Return to the pot and stir in the lemon juice. Garnish with freshly chopped cilantro if desired.

Per serving: 138 calories (0% from fat)
6 g protein; 28 g carbohydrate; 0 g fat; 198 mg sodium; 0 mg cholesterol

Potato and Corn Chowder

Serves 8

Diced green chilies add a certain warmth to this chowder. Serve it with cornbread and a green salad.

4	russet potatoes, peeled and diced (about 4 cups)
2	cups water or vegetable stock
1	yellow onion, chopped
2	garlic cloves, minced
1	red bell pepper, diced
1	teaspoon ground cumin
1	teaspoon basil
1	teaspoon salt
1/4	teaspoon black pepper
1	4-ounce can diced green chilies
2	cups corn, frozen, canned, or fresh
1-2	cups soy milk

Peel and dice the potatoes and put them in a pot with 2 cups of water or vegetable stock. Cover and cook until tender, about 20 minutes.

Heat 1/2 cup of water in a large pot and cook the onion, garlic, and bell pepper for 5 minutes. Add the cumin, basil, salt, and black pepper. Continue to cook until the onion is very soft, about 5 minutes or longer.

When the potatoes are tender, mash them in their water, and combine them with the onion mixture, along with the diced chilies, corn and 1 cup of the soy milk. Stir to blend. Add more soy milk if a thinner soup is desired. Heat gently until hot and steamy.

Per serving: 179 calories (2.5 % from fat)
          4 g protein; 40 g carbohydrate; 1 g fat; 305 mg sodium; 0 mg cholesterol

Note: For a milder soup, use only half of the chilies. Freeze the rest for later use.

Creamy Curried Carrot Soup

Serves 4

It's hard to believe that such a simple soup could be so delicious. This soup is a rich source of beta carotene.

1	**onion, coarsely chopped**
6	**carrots, sliced**
2	**cups water or vegetable stock**
1	**teaspoon curry powder**
2	**cups soy milk or rice milk**
1/2	**teaspoon salt**

Combine the onion and carrots in a pot with the water or vegetable stock and curry powder. Cover and simmer until the carrots can be easily pierced with a fork, about 20 minutes.

Puree the carrots mixture (including the liquid) in a blender in two or three small batches, adding some of the milk to each batch. Be sure to start the blender on low speed and hold the lid on tightly. The soup should be very smooth. Pour it back in the pot. If it seems too thick, add a bit more milk to achieve the desired consistency. Add salt to taste and heat gently until steamy.

Per serving: 105 calories (8% from fat)
3 g protein; 21 g carbohydrate; 1 g fat; 217 mg sodium; 0 mg cholesterol

Split Pea Soup

Serves 6 to 8

This simple one-pot soup contains no added fat, and is a perfect warm-up for a cold day. I like to make it in a crockpot, so that when I get home, the aroma of soup fills the house.

2	**cups split peas, rinsed**
6	**cups water**
1	**medium onion, chopped**
1	**cup carrots, sliced or diced**
1	**cup celery, sliced**
1	**large potato, peeled and diced**
1	**large yam, peeled and diced (optional)**
2	**garlic cloves, minced**
1/2	**teaspoon marjoram**
1/2	**teaspoon basil**
1/4	**teaspoon ground cumin**
1/4	**teaspoon black pepper**
1	**teaspoon salt**
	pinch cayenne

Combine the split peas in a large pot with the remaining ingredients. Bring to a simmer, then cover loosely and cook until the peas are tender, about 1 hour. For a thicker, more uniform soup, use a potato masher to mash some of the peas and vegetables.

Per serving: 158 calories (0% from fat)
          9 g protein; 29 g carbohydrate; 0 g fat; 282 mg sodium; 0 mg cholesterol

Crockpot method: Combine all the ingredients in a crockpot and cook on high until the peas are tender, about 6 to 8 hours. For quicker cooking, bring the water to a boil before adding it.

Borscht

Serves 6

This delicious vegetable soup can be eaten plain, or with the optional creamy topping. Serve it with rye bread and a crisp green salad.

1-2 **beets, peeled and diced (about 1 cup)**
1 **small onion chopped**
1 **medium potato, cut in 1/4-inch cubes**
1 **carrot, sliced or diced**
1 **celery stalk, thinly sliced**
1 **cup finely shredded green cabbage**
1 **15-ounce can Swanson's Vegetable Broth — OR—**
   2 cups other fat-free vegetable broth
1 **cup crushed tomatoes**
2 **cups water**
1/2 **teaspoon dill weed**
1/2 **teaspoon caraway seeds**
1/8 **teaspoon black pepper**

Optional Topping:
1/2 **cup Fat-Free Nayonaise**
5-6 **tablespoons lemon juice**

Combine everything except the topping ingredients in a large pot and bring to a simmer. Cover and cook until the beets and potatoes are tender, about 25 minutes.

To prepare the topping, mix the Nayonaise and lemon juice.

Ladle the soup into bowls. Top each bowl with 1 to 2 tablespoons of topping, if desired, and serve.

Per serving (without topping): 71 calories (0% from fat)
       2 g protein; 16 g carbohydrate; 0 g fat; 204 mg sodium; 0 mg cholesterol

Per serving (with topping): 76 calories (0% from fat)
       2 g protein; 17 g carbohydrate; 0 g fat; 224 mg sodium; 0 mg cholesterol

Golden Mushroom Soup

Serves 6

This is a rich-tasting soup, delicious with fresh baked bread, baked yams, and a green salad.

2   tablespoons soy sauce
2   medium onions, chopped
1   pound mushrooms, sliced
11/2 teaspoons dill weed
1   tablespoon paprika
1   teaspoon caraway seeds (optional)
1/8   teaspoon black pepper
1   15-ounce can Swanson's Vegetable Broth

11/2 cups soy milk or rice milk
2   teaspoons lemon juice
2-3   tablespoons red wine (optional)

Heat 1/2 cup of water in a large pot. Add the soy sauce and chopped onions and cook until the onions are soft and translucent, about 5 minutes. Add the sliced mushrooms, dill, paprika, caraway seeds, and black pepper. Cook another 5 minutes, stirring frequently. Add the vegetable broth, then cover and simmer 15 minutes.

Place 1 cup of the soup into a blender, along with the soy milk or rice milk, and blend until smooth. Return it to the pot and heat until steamy without letting it boil. Stir in the lemon juice and red wine just before serving.

Per serving: 112 calories (7% from fat)
                      5 g protein; 19 g carbohydrate; 1 g fat; 338 mg sodium; 0 mg cholesterol

Spicy Pumpkin Soup

Serves 8

This Indian soup is sweet, spicy, and creamy. You could also use pureed winter squash, yams, or sweet potatoes in place of the pumkin.

21/2   cups water or vegetable stock
1   onion chopped
2   garlic cloves, minced
1/2   teaspoon mustard seeds
1/2   teaspoon turmeric
1/2   teaspoon ginger
1/2   teaspoon ground cumin
1/4   teaspoon cinnamon
1/8   teaspoon cayenne
3/4   teaspoon salt
1   15-ounce can pumpkin — OR—
**   2 cups cooked pumpkin**
2   tablespoons maple syrup
1   tablespoon lemon juice
2   cups soy milk or rice milk
fresh cilantro (optional)

Heat 1/2 cup of the water or stock in a large pot and cook the onion and garlic until the onion is soft, about 5 minutes.

Add the spices and salt and cook 2 minutes over low heat, stirring constantly. Whisk in the remaining water or stock, the pumpkin, maple syrup, and lemon juice. Simmer 15 minutes.

Add the soy milk or rice milk and puree the soup in a blender in two to three batches until very smooth. Be sure to start on low speed and hold the lid on tightly. Return to the pot and heat without boiling, until steamy.

Serve immediately, with a sprinkling of fresh cilantro on top if desired.

Per serving: 64 calories (8% from fat)
             2 g protein; 13 g carbohydrate; 1 g fat; 226 mg sodium; 0 mg cholesterol

Autumn Stew

Serves 8

*Based on traditional Native American foods — squash, corn, and
beans — this stew is perfect for an autumn feast. Serve it with warm
bread and a crisp green salad.*

1	**tablespoon soy sauce**
1	**onion, chopped**
1	**red bell pepper, diced**
4	**large garlic cloves, minced**
1	**pound (about 4 cups diced) butternut squash**
1	**15-ounce can crushed tomatoes**
1 1/2	**teaspoons oregano**
1	**teaspoon chili powder**
1/2	**teaspoon cumin**
1/4	**teaspoon black pepper**
1	**15-ounce can kidney beans, undrained**
1	**15-ounce can corn, undrained (or 2 cups frozen corn)**

Heat 1/2 cup of water and the soy sauce in a large pot. Add the onion, bell
pepper, and garlic. Cook over medium heat until the onion is soft and
most of the water has evaporated, about 5 minutes.

Peel the squash, then cut it in half. Scoop out the seeds and discard.
Cut the squash into 1/2-cubes and add it to the cooked onions along with
the crushed tomatoes, 1 cup of water, the oregano, chili powder, cumin,
and pepper. Cover and simmer until the squash is just tender when
pierced with a fork, about 20 minutes. Add the kidney beans and corn
with their liquid and cook 5 minutes longer.

Per serving: 132 calories (4% from fat)
              5 g protein; 27 g carbohydrate; 1 g fat; 267 mg sodium; 0 mg cholesterol

Simply Wonderful Vegetable Stew

Serves 6 to 8

This delicious stew contains relatively few ingredients and is quick to prepare. Serve it with Braised Cabbage (page 85) and crusty sourdough French bread.

1	15-ounce can Swanson's Vegetable Broth
2	medium onions, chopped
2	garlic cloves, minced
1	28-ounce can crushed tomatoes
1	large green bell pepper, diced
6	medium red potatoes, unpeeled, cut into 1-inch chunks
1	teaspoon basil
1	teaspoon oregano
1	teaspoon mixed Italian herbs
1/4	teaspoon black pepper
1-2	cups green peas, fresh or frozen

Heat 1/2 cup of the vegetable broth in a large pot and cook the onions and garlic until soft, about 5 minutes.

Add the tomatoes, bell pepper, potatoes, remaining vegetable broth and seasonings. Bring to a simmer, then cover and cook, stirring frequently, until the potatoes are just tender, about 20 minutes. Add extra water, if necessary, to prevent sticking.

Stir in the peas and continue cooking until heated through.

Per serving: 156 calories (0% from fat)
       5 g protein; 33 g carbohydrate; 0 g fat; 250 mg sodium; 0 mg cholesterol

Lentil Barley Stew

Serves 8

This hearty one-step stew is delicious with a crisp green salad.

1	**cup lentils, rinsed**
1/2	**cup hulled or pearl barley**
6	**cups water or vegetable stock**
1	**onion, chopped**
1	**large russet potato, scrubbed and diced**
2	**garlic cloves, crushed or minced**
2	**carrots, diced**
2	**celery stalks, sliced**
1/2	**teaspoon oregano**
1/2	**teaspoon ground cumin**
1/4	**teaspoon red pepper flakes**
1/4	**teaspoon black pepper**
1	**teaspoon salt**

Place all the ingredients except salt into a large pot and bring to a simmer. Cover and cook, stirring occasionally, until lentils and barley are tender, about 1 hour. Add salt to taste.

Per serving: 86 calories (0% from fat)
3 g protein; 18 g carbohydrate; 0 g fat; 285 mg sodium; 0 mg cholesterol

Okefenokee Stew

Serves 6 to 8

This delicious, easy-to-prepare stew was inspired by a balmy southern evening in the Okefenokee Swamp. I wanted something with traditional southern flavors. What better than okra and black-eyed peas? I like to serve this stew with cooked brown rice.

1/2 cup red wine
1 large onion, chopped

2 celery stalks, sliced
1 green bell pepper, diced
3-4 cups sliced okra (3/4-1 pound), fresh or frozen
1 large tomato, diced —OR—
  1 15-ounce can crushed tomatoes
2 teaspoons chili powder
2 teaspoons oregano
1 tablespoon soy sauce

1 15-ounce can black-eyed peas, with liquid
2 cups frozen corn

cooked brown rice for serving (optional)

Heat the wine in a large pot and cook the onion until it is tender, about 5 minutes.

Add the celery, bell pepper, okra, tomato, chili powder, oregano, and soy sauce. Lower the heat, then cover and simmer for 10 minutes.

Add the black-eyed peas and corn and simmer about 10 minutes longer.

Per serving: 126 calories (0% from fat)
         5 g protein; 24 g carbohydrate; 0 g fat; 324 mg sodium; 0 mg cholesterol

VEGETABLES

Broccoli with Fat-Free Dressing

4 to 6 servings

I have always had a difficult time getting my parents to eat vegetables, especially broccoli. I've tried hiding it in soups , stir-fries, and casseroles, all with only limited success. So you can imagine my delight when I prepared this easy recipe and served it to them, and they actually liked it. Hopefully, it will be as well received by the picky vegetable eaters in your life!

1	**bunch broccoli**
1/4	**cup seasoned rice vinegar**
1	**teaspoon stoneground mustard**
1	**garlic clove, pressed or minced**

Break the broccoli into bite-sized flowerets. Peel the stems and slice them into 1/4-inch thick rounds. Steam until just tender, about 5 minutes.

While the broccoli is steaming, whisk the dressing ingredients in a serving bowl. Add the steamed broccoli and toss to mix. Serve immediately.

Per serving: 32 calories (0% from fat)
1.5 g protein; 6 g carbohydrate; 0 g fat; 216 mg sodium; 0 mg cholesterol

Variation: For a tasty salad, plunge the steamed broccoli into ice water until it is completely chilled, then toss it with the dressing.

Braised Kale or Collard Greens

Makes 2 cups

Kale and collard greens are excellent sources of calcium and beta-carotene. They are somewhat more robust in flavor than spinach, and are delicious with garlic and a bit of soy sauce. Try to purchase young tender greens, as these have the best flavor and texture.

- **1   bunch kale or collard greens (6 to 8 cups chopped)**
- **2-3 teaspoons soy sauce**
- **3-4 garlic cloves, minced**

Rinse the kale or collards. Remove the stems and chop the leaves into half-inch wide strips. Heat 1/2 cup of water in a large pot or skillet, then add the soy sauce and garlic. Cook 1 minute, then add the greens. Toss to mix, then cover and cook over medium heat until the greens are tender, 3 to 5 minutes. Stir occasionally while the greens are cooking and add a small amount of water if they begin to stick.

Per 1/2 cup: 61 calories (0% from fat)
              3 g protein; 11 g carbohydrate; 0 g fat; 101 mg sodium; 0 mg cholesterol

Braised Cabbage

Serves 2 to 3

Brasised cabbage has a delicious, sweet flavor — great with any meal.

- **2   cups green cabbage, coarsely chopped**
- **1/2 teaspoon caraway seeds (optional)**
- **salt and black pepper**

Bring about 1/2 cup of water to a boil in a skillet or saucepan. Stir in cabbage and caraway seeds if desired. Cover and cook until the cabbage is just tender, about 5 minutes. Sprinkle with salt and pepper to taste.

Per serving: 16 calories (0% from fat)
              0.5 g protein; 4 g carbohydrate; 0 g fat; 80 mg of sodium; 0 mg cholesterol

Beets with Mustard Dill Dressing

Serves 4

Try these, even if you don't like beets. You'll be amazed at how tasty they are. Serve them hot or chilled.

4   medium beets

2   tablespoons lemon juice
1   tablespoon stoneground mustard
1   tablespoon cider vinegar
1   teaspoon sugar or other sweetener
1   teaspoon dried dill — OR— 1 tablespoon fresh dill

Wash the beets and cut off the tops (save these to steam for another meal). Peel the beets, then slice them into 1/4-inch thick rounds. Steam over boiling water until tender, about 20 minutes.

Combine the lemon juice, mustard, vinegar, sugar, and dill for the dressing. Stir to mix then pour over the cooked beets. Toss and serve immediately, or chill and serve cold.

Per serving: 31 calories (0% from fat)
          1 g protein; 5 g carbohydrate; 0 g fat; 115 mg sodium; 0 mg cholesterol

Green Beans with Braised Onions

Serves 6

Green beans take on a slightly Asian flair in this simple recipe.

- 1   **pound fresh green beans (about 3 cups)**
- 1   **medium-small yellow onion, cut into thin crescents**
- 1   **tablespoon soy sauce**
- 1   **tablespoon seasoned rice vinegar**

Trim the beans and break them into bite-sized pieces. Steam until just tender, about 10 minutes.

In a large skillet heat 1/3 cup of water, then add the onions. Cook over medium heat until soft, 3 to 5 minutes. Lower the heat and add the soy sauce and seasoned rice vinegar. Continue cooking until most of the liquid has evaporated and the onion slices are lightly browned and sweet. Add the steamed beans, toss to mix, and serve.

Per serving: 36 calories (0% from fat)
2 g protein; 7 g carbohydrate; 0 g fat; 105 mg sodium; 0 mg cholesterol

Italian Green Beans

Serves 6

1   pound fresh green beans, trimmed (about 3 cups)

1   tablespoon soy sauce
4   large garlic cloves, minced
1   15-ounce can crushed tomatoes
2   tablespoons chopped fresh basil — OR—
  1 teaspoon dried basil
1/4 teaspoon black pepper

Trim the beans and break them into bite-sized pieces.   Steam until just tender, about 10 minutes.

In a large skillet, heat 1/4 cup of water, then add the soy sauce and minced garlic and cook over medium heat for 1 minute. Add the tomatoes, basil, and pepper and simmer uncovered over medium heat for 3 to 5 minutes. Stir in the cooked beans, and cook 2 to 3 more minutes.

Per serving: 48 calories (0% from fat)
           2 g protein; 10 g carbohydrate; 0 g fat; 220 mg sodium; 0 mg cholesterol

Oven Fries

Serves 6

Be sure to try this simple, fat-free version of French fries!

4   **medium large potatoes**
1   **teaspoon garlic granules or powder**
1   **teaspoon mixed Italian herbs**
1/2   **teaspoon paprika or chili powder**
1/4   **teaspoon salt**
      black pepper

Preheat the oven to 450°F. Scrub the potatoes and cut them into "fries". Place in a large mixing bowl and sprinkle with the garlic granules, Italian herbs, paprika or chili powder, salt, and pepper. Toss to mix.

Line two 9 x 13-inch baking dishes with baking parchment or foil (this makes the clean-up much easier). Arrange the potatoes in a single layer in the baking dishes. Bake in the preheated oven until tender when pierced with a fork, about 30 minutes.

Per serving: 147 calories (0% from fat)
          2 g protein; 34 g carbohydrate; 0 g fat; 100 mg sodium; 0 mg cholesterol

Variation: Small new potatoes, like "Yellow Finns," or "Yukon Gold" are also delicious when prepared in this way. Simply scrub about 5 cups of new potatoes but do not peel them. Small potatoes (up to 1 inch in diameter) can be cooked whole. Cut larger potatoes into 1-inch chunks.

Curried Potatoes

Serves 6

Top these colorful, spicy potatoes with chutney and serve them with a lentil or bean soup.

4	**large red potatoes**
2	**teaspoons whole mustard seed**
1/2	**teaspoon turmeric**
1/2	**teaspoon cumin**
1/4	**teaspoon ginger**
1/8	**teaspoon cayenne**
1/8	**teaspoon black pepper**
1	**onion, chopped**
1 1/2	**teaspoons soy sauce**

Scrub the potatoes, then cut them into 1/2-inch cubes. Steam them until tender when pierced with a fork, 20 to 25 minutes. Cool completely.

Toast the spices in a large, dry nonstick skillet for 1 to 2 minutes, stirring constantly. Carefully pour in 1/2 cup of water (there will be some splattering). Add the chopped onion and cook, stirring frequently, until it is soft and most of the liquid has evaporated, about 5 minutes.

Add the cooled potatoes along with another 1/2 cup of water. Stir in the soy sauce, then cover and cook over medium heat for 5 minutes. Stir before serving.

Per serving: 161 calories (0% from fat)
            3 g protein; 37 g carbohydrate; 0 g fat; 62 mg of sodium; 0 mg cholesterol

Oven Roasted Yams

Serves 8

Oven roasting is a quick and delicious way to prepare yams. The high heat seals in flavor and moisture as it crisps the outside edges. For the best result, be sure to arrange the yams in a single layer in the pans.

4	**medium yams (jewel and garnet work well)**
1	**teaspoon garlic granules or powder**
1	**teaspoon mixed Italian herbs**
1/4	**teaspoon salt**
	black pepper

Preheat the oven to 450°F. Scrub the yams and cut them into 1-inch chunks. Place them in a large mixing bowl and sprinkle them with the garlic granules, Italian herbs, salt, and pepper.

Line two 9 x 13-inch baking dishes with baking parchment or foil (this makes clean-up easier). Arrange the yams in a single layer in the baking dishes. Bake in the preheated oven until tender when pierced with a fork, 25 to 30 minutes.

Per serving: 158 calories (0% from fat)
1.5 g protein; 38 g carbohydrate; 0 g fat; 100 mg sodium; 0 mg cholesterol

Grilled Summer Vegetables

Serves 8

Grilled vegetables are easy to prepare and delicious as a side dish with polenta, pasta, or rice. The vegetables can be varied according to the season and your tastes. For example, use fresh asparagus when it is available in spring, and zucchini during summer and fall.

1	**large red onion**
1	**large red bell pepper**
1	**pound fresh asparagus — OR — 2 medium zucchini**
2-3	**cups button mushrooms**
2	**ears fresh corn**
2	**teaspoons garlic granules or powder**
2	**teaspoons mixed Italian herbs**
2	**teaspoons chili powder**
1/2	**teaspoon salt**

While the grill preheats, cut the onion, bell pepper, and zucchini (if using) into generous bite-sized pieces. Place in a large mixing bowl. Clean the mushrooms and add them to the bowl. Break or cut the tough ends off the asparagus, then break or cut it into 1-inch lengths and add it to the bowl. Husk the corn and cut it into 1 to 2-inch lengths. Add it to the bowl. Combine the garlic granules, Italian herbs, chili powder and salt and sprinkle them over the vegetables. Toss to mix.

Spread a single layer of the vegetables on a grill rack (one with small holes is helpful for keeping the vegetables out of the coals). Place over medium-hot coals, cover and grill. After about 5 minutes, turn the vegetables with a spatula, then cover and grill until they are tender when pierced with a sharp knife, about 5 more minutes. Repeat with remaining vegetables.

Per serving: 44 calories (0% from fat)
2 g protein; 9 g carbohydrate; 0 g fat; 138 mg sodium; 0 mg cholesterol

Easy Yams with Pineapple

Serves 8

This is absolutely one of the easiest and most delicious ways to prepare yams!

5   medium yams or sweet potatoes, unpeeled
1   15-ounce can crushed pineapple in juice

Scrub the yams or sweet potatoes and steam them over boiling water until tender, about 25 minutes. Remove from steamer and cool slightly. When they are cool enough to handle, cut a lengthwise slit in each yam and squeeze the ends to open it. Leaving the flesh in the skin, use a fork to mash it slightly. Mix in 2 to 3 tablespoons of the undrained crushed pineapple, then fill each of the cavities with the remaining pineapple.

Another way to prepare these is to peel the cooked yams when they are cool enough to handle, then mash the flesh and mix in all of the pineapple, including the liquid.

Per serving: 177 calories (0% from fat)
          1.5 g protein; 42 g carbohydrate; 0 g fat; 11 mg sodium; 0 mg cholesterol

Simply Wonderful Winter Squash

Makes 4 cups

In spite of its name, winter squash is available year round in most places. If you've never tried a butternut, kabocha, or delicata you're in for a real treat, because they're absolutely delicious. Be sure to try this easy recipe for starters.

1	**winter squash (butternut, kabocha, etc.)**
2	**teaspoons soy sauce**
2	**tablespoons maple syrup**

Cut the squash in half, then peel it and remove the seeds. Cut the squash into 1-inch cubes (you should have about 4 cups). Place into a large pot with 1/2 cup of water. Add the soy sauce and maple syrup. Cover and simmer over medium heat until the squash is fork tender, 15 to 20 minutes.

Per 1 cup: 92 calories (6% from fat)
            2 g protein; 19 g carbohydrate; 1 g fat; 102 mg sodium; 0 mg cholesterol

Grilled Winter Squash

Serves 4

1	**medium winter squash (butternut, kabocha, etc.)**
2	**tablespoons maple syrup**
2	**teaspoons soy sauce**

Peel the squash if desired then cut it in half and remove the seeds. Slice the squash into 1/2-inch thick strips and steam over boiling water until just tender when pierced with a sharp knife.

Mix the maple syrup and soy sauce in a small bowl.

Brush or spray the grill with vegetable oil and arrange the cooked squash slices on it. Baste with the maple syrup mixture. Grill over medium-hot coals, turning and basting frequently, until the outsides are pleasantly browned, about 10 minutes.

Per serving: 72 calories (0% from fat)
1 g protein; 17 g carbohydrate; 0 g fat; 92 mg sodium; 0 mg cholesterol

Roasted Red Peppers

Makes two roasted peppers

Roasted red peppers are delicious additions to salads, vegetables dishes, and sauces. They freeze nicely for easy use any time.

2   fresh red bell peppers

Place peppers over an open flame (such as a gas burner on the stove) or under the oven broiler. Turn with tongs until the skin is charred on all sides. Place in a bowl, and cover with a plate until cool enough to handle, about 15 minutes, then peel off the charred skin with your fingers. Cut the peppers in half, saving any juice which drains out, and remove the seeds.

Per pepper: 18 calories (0% from fat)
     0.5 g protein; 4 g carbohydrate; 0 g fat; 2 mg sodium; 0 mg cholesterol

Tip: Roasted red peppers packed in water are sold in most supermarkets. Look for them near the pickles.

Roasted Garlic

Roasted garlic makes a delicious appetizer, or accompaniment to a meal. I place several heads on the table and enjoy watching people discover the mild taste and creamy texture. Roasted garlic can also be used as a spread on bread, or in salads and dressings. Store it in a sealed container in the refrigerator for up to 2 weeks.

Start with a firm head of garlic which has nice large cloves. Place it in a small baking dish and bake it in a conventional or toaster oven at 375°F until the cloves feel soft when pressed, about 25 minutes.

Per head: 40 calories (0% from fat)
     0 g protein; 10 g carbohydrate; 0 g fat; 10 mg sodium; 0 mg cholesterol

GRAINS & SIDE DISHES

Brown Rice

Makes 3 cups of cooked rice

Brown rice supplies more vitamins, minerals, protein, and fiber than white rice. Cooking it in extra water ensures perfect rice and actually reduces the cooking time.

Short grain brown rice tends to be a bit chewier, while long grain brown rice is slightly more tender and fluffy. If you are new to brown rice, I would recommend starting with the long grain variety.

1   cup short or long grain brown rice
4   cups water
1/2   teaspoon salt

Rinse and drain the rice. Bring the water to a boil in a saucepan, then add the rice and salt. Once the water returns to a boil, lower the heat slightly, then cover loosely and boil gently about 40 minutes, until the rice is soft but still retains a hint of crunchiness. Pour off any excess liquid (this can be saved and used as a broth for soups and stews if desired).

Per 1/2 cup: 115 calories (4% from fat)
          2.5 g protein; 25 g carbohydrate; 1 g fat; 176 mg sodium; 0 mg cholesterol

Quick Confetti Rice

Makes about 3 cups

This colorful rice pilaf has no added fat, so be sure to use a nonstick pan.

2	cups cooked brown rice
1/2	cup frozen corn
1/2	cup frozen peas
1/2	cup diced red bell pepper
1/2	teaspoon curry powder
1/4	cup raisins (optional)

salt to taste

Prepare brown rice according to the recipe on the preceding page. Heat 1/4 cup of water in a large skillet. Add the cooked rice, using a spatula to separate the rice kernels. Add the corn, peas, bell pepper, curry powder, and raisins. Heat thoroughly. Add salt to taste.

Per 1/2 cup: 109 calories (0% from fat)
2.5 g protein; 24 g carbohydrate; 0 g fat; 112 mg sodium; 0 mg cholesterol

Simply Spanish Rice

Makes about 3 cups

2	teaspoons chili powder
1	teaspoon garlic granules or powder
1/2	teaspoon ground cumin
1/4	teaspoon salt
1	tablespoon soy sauce
1	cup uncooked long-grain brown rice

Mix the chili powder, garlic granules, cumin, salt, and soy sauce with 2 cups of water in a saucepan. Stir in the rice. Bring to a simmer, then cover loosely and cook until the rice is tender, about 45 minutes. Add a small amount of additional water if the rice begins to stick before it is done.

Per 1/2 cup serving: 104 calories (0% from fat)
2 g protein; 23 g carbohydrate; 0 g fat; 200 mg sodium; 0 mg cholesterol

Wild Basmati Pilaf

Serves 6

The combination of wild rice (which is not a true rice) and basmati rice give this pilaf marvelous flavor and texture without added fat. Wild rice and basmati rice are available in natural food stores and in some supermarkets.

1/4	**cup wild rice**
1	**15-ounce can Swanson's Vegetable Broth**
3/4	**cup brown basmati rice**
1	**onion, finely chopped**
3	**garlic cloves, minced**
2	**cups thinly sliced mushrooms**
2	**celery stalks, thinly sliced**
1/2	**teaspoon thyme**
1/2	**teaspoon marjoram**
1/4	**teaspoon black pepper**
1/4	**teaspoon salt**
1/3	**cup finely chopped parsley**

Rinse the wild rice and place it in a saucepan with the vegetable broth. Stir to mix, then cover and simmer for 20 minutes. Add the basmati rice and 1/2 cup of water. Cover and continue cooking until both varieties of rice are tender, about 50 minutes.

Heat 1/2 cup of water in a large pot or skillet. Add the onion and garlic and cook until the water has evaporated and bits of onion begin to stick to the pan. Add another 1/4 cup of water, scraping the pan to remove any pieces of onion. Cook until the water evaporates again, stirring occasionally. Repeat this process until the onions are browned. This will take about 15 minutes. Add the mushrooms, celery, and seasonings. Cook, stirring frequently, for 5 minutes, then add the cooked rice and chopped parsley. Cook over low heat, turning gently, until very hot.

Per serving: 124 calories (7% from fat)
3 g protein; 27 g carbohydrate; 1 g fat; 284 mg sodium; 0 mg cholesterol

Bulgur

Makes about 2 1/2 cups

Bulgur is cracked wheat which has been toasted to give it a delicious, nutty flavor. It cooks in about 15 minutes and is an excellent accompaniment to a wide variety of foods, from chili to roasted vegetables.

1   cup bulgur
1/2   teaspoon salt

Bring 2 cups of water to a boil in a saucepan, then stir in bulgur and salt. Reduce the heat to a simmer, then cover and cook without stirring until the bulgur is tender and all the water is absorbed, about 15 minutes. Fluff with a fork.

Per 1/2 cup: 113 calories (0% from fat)
          4 g protein; 24 g carbohydrate; 0 g fat; 216 mg sodium; 0 mg cholesterol

Variation: Combine bulgur and salt in a pan or mixing bowl, then stir in 2 cups of boiling water. Cover and let stand until all the water is absorbed, about 25 minutes. Use this "cooking" method whenever you want especially loose, fluffy bulgur.

Couscous

Makes 3 cups

Couscous cooks in minutes and makes a delicious side dish or salad ingredient.

1/2   teaspoon salt
1   cup couscous

Bring 1 1/2 cups of water to a boil, then stir in the salt and couscous. Remove from the heat and cover. Let stand 10 to 15 minutes, then fluff with a fork and serve.

Per 1/2 cup: 91 calories (0% from fat)
          3 g protein; 20 g carbohydrate; 0 g fat; 93 mg sodium; 0 mg cholesterol

Polenta

Makes about 11/2 cups

Polenta is a coarse cornmeal porridge that has long been a dietary staple in northern Italy. It cooks easily and is delicious topped with marinara or any spicy sauce. It can also be chilled, then sliced and grilled, as described below.

1/2   cup polenta
1   15-ounce can Swanson's Vegetable Broth

Combine the polenta, vegetable broth, and 1/2 cup of water in a pan. Bring to a simmer and cook, stirring frequently, until very thick. This will take 15 to 20 minutes. Top with the sauce of your choice.

For grilled polenta, pour the cooked hot polenta into a 9 x 9-inch ungreased baking dish and chill completely. Cut into squares and cook in one of the following ways:

- grill over medium-hot coals on an oil-sprayed rack
- broil in the oven on an oil-sprayed baking sheet
- saute in an oil-sprayed nonstick skillet.

Per 1/2-cup serving: 88 calories (0% from fat)
      2 g protein; 18 g carbohydrate; 0 g fat; 350 mg sodium; 0 mg cholesterol

Variation: For Rosemary Polenta, add 1 teaspoon of crushed rosemary to the above recipe.

Zucchini Corn Fritters

Makes 16 fritters

These "fritters" are not deep fried, but actually cooked like pancakes.

11/3 **cups soy milk**
1   **tablespoon cider vinegar**

1   **cup cornmeal**
1/4   **cup unbleached flour**
1/2   **teaspoon baking powder**
1/2   **teaspoon baking soda**
1/2   **teaspoon salt**
1   **medium zucchini (about 1 cup grated or finely chopped)**
1   **cup corn (fresh, frozen, or canned)**

Combine the soy milk and vinegar and set aside.

In a mixing bowl, combine the cornmeal, flour, baking powder, baking soda, and salt.

Chop or grate the zucchini (a food processor makes it easy), then add it to the cornmeal mixture along with the soy milk mixture and corn. Stir to mix.

Heat a nonstick skillet and spray it with vegetable oil spray. Pour small amounts of batter into the pan and cook the first side until the edges are dry, about 2 minutes. Carefully turn the fritters and cook the second side until browned, about 1 minute.

Per fritter: 55 calories (0% from fat)
            2 g protein; 11 g carbohydrate; 0 g fat; 101 mg sodium; 0 mg cholesterol

Traditional Bread Dressing

Serves 6

Now you can enjoy traditional dressing again, because it's fat-free!

1	onion, chopped
3	cups sliced mushrooms (about 1/2 pound)
2	celery stalks, thinly sliced
4	cups cubed bread
1/3	cup finely chopped parsley
1/2	teaspoon thyme
1/2	teaspoon marjoram
1/2	teaspoon sage
1/2	teaspoon salt
1/8	teaspoon black pepper
1	cup (approximately) hot water or vegetable stock

Heat 1/2 cup of water in a large pot or skillet. Add the onion and cook for 5 minutes. Add the sliced mushrooms and celery and cook over medium heat, stirring occasionally, for another 5 minutes.

Preheat the oven to 350°F. Stir the bread into the onion mixture, along with the parsley, thyme, marjoram, sage, salt, and black pepper. Lower the heat and continue cooking for 3 minutes, then stir in the water or stock, a little at a time, until the dressing obtains the desired moistness. Spread in an oil-sprayed baking dish, cover and bake for 20 minutes. Remove the cover and bake 10 minutes longer.

Per serving: 102 calories (8% from fat)
          4 g protein; 19 g carbohydrate; 1 g fat; 396 mg sodium; 0 mg cholesterol

Mashed Potatoes and Gravy

Serves 8

Now you can enjoy this traditional favorite to your heart's content!

4	**large russet potatoes, peeled and diced**
1/2	**teaspoon salt**
1/2-1	**cup soy milk or rice milk**

1	**tablespoon soy sauce**
1/2	**cup finely chopped onion**
1	**cup sliced mushrooms**

2	**tablespoons flour**
1/4	**teaspoon garlic granules or powder**
1/4	**teaspoon poultry seasoning**
1/8	**teaspoon black pepper**

Combine the potatoes with 2 cups of water and the salt in a saucepan. Simmer until tender when pierced with a fork, about 10 minutes. Drain, reserving the liquid, then mash the potatoes, adding enough milk to achieve a creamy consistency. Add salt to taste. Cover and set aside.

Heat 1/2 cup of water and the soy sauce in a large skillet, then add the onion and mushrooms. Cover and cook over medium heat 5 minutes, stirring occasionally.

Mix the flour with 1/2 cup of water and add it to the onions along with the seasonings and reserved potato water. Stir over medium heat until thickened, then serve with the mashed potatoes.

Per serving: 134 calories (0% from fat)
             3 g protein; 30 g carbohydrate; 0 g fat; 228 mg sodium; 0 mg cholesterol

Variation: If you prefer smooth gravy, puree it in a blender.

Spinach and Bread Pudding

Serves 6

This savory bread pudding topped with the Quick Garbanzo Gravy on the following page is hearty enough to be a meal.

1	**batch Quick Garbanzo Gravy (next page)**
1	**large onion, chopped**
3	**cups sliced mushrooms (about 1/2 pound)**
2	**celery stalks, thinly sliced**
1	**cup finely chopped green cabbage**
1/3	**cup finely chopped parsley**
3/4	**teaspoon thyme**
3/4	**teaspoon marjoram**
3/4	**teaspoon sage**
1/2	**teaspoon garlic granules or powder**
1/2	**teaspoon salt**
1/4	**teaspoon black pepper**
5-6	**cups cubed bread**
1	**10-ounce package frozen chopped spinach, thawed**
1	**cup (approximately) hot water or vegetable stock**

Heat 1/2 cup of water in a large pot, then add the onion and cook over high heat, stirring occasionally, for 5 minutes. Add the sliced mushrooms, celery, cabbage, thyme, marjoram, sage, garlic granules, salt, and pepper. Cover and cook over medium heat, stirring occasionally, until the mushrooms begin to darken, about 10 minutes.

Add the bread cubes, thawed spinach, and enough hot water or stock to lightly moisten the bread. Stir to mix, then continue cooking over medium-low heat until heated through, about 5 minutes. Serve with Quick Garbanzo Gravy.

Per serving (with gravy): 231 calories (8% from fat)
          10 g protein; 42 g carbohydrate; 2 g fat; 590 mg sodium; 0 mg cholesterol

Per serving (without gravy): 143 calories (8% from fat)
          6 g protein; 27 g carbohydrate; 1 g fat; 388 mg sodium; 0 mg cholesterol

Quick Garbanzo Gravy

Makes about 2 cups

1	**cup chopped onion**
1	**tablespoon soy sauce**
1	**15-ounce can garbanzo beans, undrained**
1/4	**teaspoon poultry seasoning**

Heat 1/2 cup of water in a large skillet, then add the onion and soy sauce. Cook over high heat, stirring frequently, until the liquid has evaporated. Add another 1/2 cup of water and continue cooking until it too has evaporated. Add 1/4 cup of water, stirring to remove any pieces of onion from the pan, then transfer the contents of the skillet to a blender. Add the garbanzo beans with their liquid, the poultry seasoning, and 1 cup of water. Blend until completely smooth. Return to the skillet, and gently heat, stirring occasionally.

Per 1/4-cup serving: 88 calories (10% from fat)
        4 g protein; 15 g carbohydrate; 1 g fat; 212 mg sodium; 0 mg cholesterol

Mushroom Gravy

Makes about 11/2 cups

1	**tablespoon soy sauce**
1	**cup finely chopped onion**
2	**cups sliced mushrooms**
2	**tablespoons whole wheat pastry flour**
1/2	**teaspoon garlic granules or powder**
1/4	**teaspoon poultry seasoning**
1/4	**teaspoon Spike or other vegetable seasoning salt**
1/8	**teaspoon black pepper**

Heat 1/2 cup of water and the soy sauce in a large skillet. Add the onion and mushrooms. Cover and cook over high heat 10 minutes, stirring often. Mix the flour with 2 cups of water and add it to the cooked onion mixture along with the seasonings. Stir constantly over medium heat until thick. For a smooth gravy, puree it in a blender.

Per 1/4-cup serving: 25 calories (0% from fat)
        1 g protein; 5 g carbohydrate; 0 g fat; 190 mg sodium; 0 mg cholesterol

MAIN DISHES

Thai Vegetables with Rice

Serves 8

This dish is colorful and mildly spicy. Serve it with flavorful basmati or jasmine rice.

2	tablespoons soy sauce
1	onion, thinly sliced
4	garlic cloves, minced
2	yams, peeled and cut into strips (about 1 pound)
1	15-ounce can crushed tomatoes
2	teaspoons ground coriander
1	teaspoon ground cumin
1/2-1	teaspoon red pepper flakes
1/2	teaspoon turmeric
1/2	teaspoon ginger powder — OR—
	2 teaspoons fresh ginger, minced or grated
1	15-ounce can garbanzo beans, including liquid
21/2	cups diced zucchini (about 1 pound)
1	red bell pepper, cut into thin strips
2	teaspoons grated lemon peel (lemon zest)
1	tablespoon lemon juice
6	cups cooked basmati or jasmine rice (2 cups raw)

Heat 1/2 cup of water and the soy sauce in a large pot. Add the onion and garlic and cook 5 minutes. Add the yams, tomatoes, coriander, cumin, pepper flakes, turmeric, ginger, and another 1/2 cup of water. Cover and simmer until the yams are just barely tender, about 15 minutes.

Add the garbanzo beans with their liquid, the zucchini, bell pepper, and grated lemon peel. Cover and simmer until the zucchini is just tender, about 5 minutes. Stir in the lemon juice. Serve with cooked rice.

Per serving: 286 calories (3% from fat)
7 g protein; 62 g carbohydrate; 1 g fat; 166 mg sodium; 0 mg cholesterol

Sweet and Sour Stir-fry

Serves 6

1/3   **cup ketchup**
3   **tablespoons vinegar**
3   **tablespoons brown sugar**
1   **tablespoon soy sauce**
1   **tablespoon cornstarch**
pinch cayenne

1   **small onion, chopped or thinly sliced into half-moons**
2   **garlic cloves, crushed**
2   **cups sliced mushrooms**
1   **stalk celery, thinly sliced**
1   **red bell pepper, thinly sliced**
1   **medium zucchini, thinly sliced**
1   **cup thinly sliced green cabbage**
2   **cups snow peas**

3-4   **cups cooked rice (1 cup uncooked)**

Combine the ketchup, vinegar, brown sugar, soy sauce, cornstarch, cayenne, and 1/2 cup of water in a bowl. Stir to mix, then set aside.

In a large skillet or wok, heat 1/2 cup of water. Add the onion and garlic and cook over high heat, stirring often, until the onion begins to soften, about 3 minutes.

Add the mushrooms and celery, cook 3 minutes, then add the bell pepper, zucchini, and cabbage. Continue cooking over high heat, stirring continuously, until the vegetables are just tender, about 3 more minutes.

Stir in the snow peas and sauce. Cook, stirring constantly, until the sauce is clear and thickened, about 2 minutes. Serve with cooked rice.

Per serving: 184 calories (3% from fat)
                5 g protein; 40 g carbohydrate; 1 g fat; 122 mg sodium; 0 mg cholesterol

Fast Lane Chow Mein

Serves 4

This chow mein takes just minutes to prepare and is a delicious way to load up on nutritious vegetables. Ramen soups are sold in natural food stores and many supermarkets. Be sure to choose a vegetarian brand in which the noodles are baked rather than fried: Westbrae and Soken are two such brands.

1	**onion, chopped**
4-5	**garlic cloves, minced**
1	**celery stalk, thinly sliced**
2 1/2	**cups sliced mushrooms**
1	**cup thinly sliced green cabbage**
2	**cups chopped kale or broccoli flowerets**
2	**packages vegetarian ramen soup (I use Westbrae Miso Ramen)**

Heat 1/2 cup of water in a large pot. Add the chopped onion and garlic. Cook until the onion is soft, about 5 minutes.

Add the celery, mushrooms, cabbage, and kale or broccoli. Break the ramen noodles into pieces (I use the handle of my knife to do this) and add them to the vegetable mixture along with **one** of the ramen seasoning packets and 1 cup of water. Stir to mix, then cover and cook over medium-high heat until the vegetables and noodles are tender, about 5 to 7 minutes. Stir occasionally during this time and add small amounts of additional water if needed to prevent sticking.

Per serving: 228 calories (7% from fat)
7 g protein; 45 g carbohydrate; 2 g fat; 394 mg sodium; 0 mg cholesterol

Roasted Vegetables with Pasta

Serves 6 to 8

What a happy coincidence that the easiest way to cook vegetables is also the tastiest. Oven-roasting vegetables takes only minutes and brings out their very best flavor.

8	**ounces pasta**
3	**summer squash (zucchini, crookneck, etc.)**
1	**large red onion**
1	**large red bell pepper, seeded**
2	**cups small, firm mushrooms**
1/2	**pound very firm tofu, cut into 1/2-inch cubes (optional)**
1	**teaspoon garlic granules or powder**
1	**teaspoon mixed Italian herbs**
1	**teaspoon chili powder**
1/4	**teaspoon salt**
1/4	**teaspoon black pepper**
2	**tomatoes, diced**

Cook the pasta in boiling water until it is just tender. Drain and rinse.

Preheat the oven to 500°F. Cut the squash, red onion, and bell pepper into generous 1-inch chunks and place in a large bowl. Clean the mushrooms and add them to the bowl. Add the tofu cubes if desired. Sprinkle with the garlic granules, Italian herbs, chili powder, salt, and pepper. Toss gently to mix. Line one or two baking sheets with baking parchment or foil and spread the vegetable mixture in a single layer. Bake in the preheated oven until tender, about 10 minutes.

Spread the cooked pasta on a large serving platter. Top with the roasted vegetables and the diced tomatoes. Serve immediately.

Per serving: 172 calories (8% from fat)
         10 g protein; 29 g carbohydrate; 1.5 g fat; 84 mg sodium; 0 mg cholesterol

Variation: When the weather permits, cooking the vegetables on a grill makes them even more flavorful.

Hearty Chili Mac

Serves 8

*The notion of combining pasta and chili was not my own, and in fact,
I prepared my first test batch with reluctance. So I was delightfully
surprised when everyone who tried it, myself included, responded with
enthusiasm and requests for seconds. I hope you, too, will enjoy this
recipe.*

8	ounces pasta spirals
1	onion, chopped
3	garlic cloves, minced
1	small red or green bell pepper, diced
2 1/2	cups Harvest Burger for Recipes — OR —
	4 Boca Burgers, thawed and chopped
1	15-ounce can crushed tomatoes
1	15-ounce can kidney beans, including liquid
1	15-ounce can corn, including liquid
2	tablespoons chili powder
1	teaspoon ground cumin
1/4	teaspoon salt

Cook the pasta in boiling water until it is tender. Drain and rinse,
then set it aside.

Heat 1/2 cup of water in a large pot then add the chopped onion and
garlic. Cook until the onion is soft, about 5 minutes. Add the bell
pepper and Harvest Burger or chopped Boca Burgers. Mix in the
crushed tomatoes, kidney beans, corn, chili powder, cumin, and salt.
Cover and simmer over medium heat, stirring occasionally, for
20 minutes. Add the cooked pasta and check the seasonings. Add
more chili powder if a spicier dish is desired.

Per serving: 190 calories (0% from fat)
12 g protein; 34 g carbohydrate; 0 g fat; 442 mg sodium; 0 mg cholesterol

Shepherd's Pie

Serves 8

This is a hearty and satisfying vegetable stew with a top "crust" of fluffy mashed potatoes.

4	**large russet potatoes, diced**
1/2-1	**cup soy milk**
1/2	**teaspoon salt**
1/2	**cup water or vegetable stock**
2	**onions, chopped**
1	**large green or red bell pepper, diced**
2	**carrots, sliced**
2	**stalks of celery, sliced**
1/2	**pound (about 2 cups) mushrooms, sliced**
1	**15-ounce can crushed tomatoes**
1	**15-ounce can kidney beans, drained**
1	**teaspoon paprika**
1/2	**teaspoon black pepper**
2	**tablespoons soy sauce**

Dice the potatoes and steam until tender. Mash, adding enough soy milk to make them smooth and spreadable. Add salt to taste. Set aside.

In a large pot, heat the water or stock. Add the chopped onions and cook 5 minutes. Add the pepper, carrots, and celery and continue cooking over medium heat another 5 minutes. Add the mushrooms, then cover the pan and cook 7 minutes, stirring occasionally. Add the tomatoes, kidney beans, paprika, pepper, and soy sauce. Cover and cook 10 minutes.

Pour the vegetables into a 9 x 13-inch baking dish and spread the mashed potatoes evenly over the top. Sprinkle with paprika. Bake at 350°F for 25 minutes, until hot and bubbly.

Per serving: 272 calories (0% from fat)
        8 g protein; 58 g carbohydrate; 0 g fat; 301 mg sodium; 0 mg cholesterol

Holiday Tofu Roast

Serves 8

Although this recipe doesn't qualify as "quick and easy," I've included it because it makes such a delicious, fat-free centerpiece for holiday meals. It is particularly good with Mushroom Gravy (page 106).

1	tablespoon soy sauce
1	onion, chopped
3	cups sliced mushrooms
1	cup sliced celery
1/2	cup finely chopped parsley
5-6	cups bread cubes
2	teaspoons poultry seasoning
1/4	teaspoon salt
1/4	teaspoon black pepper
1	cup water or vegetable stock
1 1/2	pounds firm tofu
2	tablespoons cornstarch
2	teaspoons Spike seasoning or other vegetable salt
1/4	teaspoon black pepper

Heat 1/2 cup of water and the soy sauce in a large pot, then add the onion and cook 3 minutes. Add the mushrooms and celery, then cover and cook over medium heat for 5 minutes. Stir in the parsley, bread, and seasonings. Add enough water or vegetable stock to moisten the dressing (about 1 cup should be sufficient).

Puree the tofu, cornstarch, Spike, and pepper in a food processor until completely smooth. Coat a large bread pan with oil-spray then dust it with flour. Spread a layer of the tofu mixture on the bottom and sides of the pan, reserving about 1 cup for the top. Fill the cavity with dressing and spread the remaining tofu mixture over the top. Cover the pan with a baking sheet or foil, and bake in a 350°F oven for 40 minutes. Uncover and continue baking 10 minutes. Remove from the oven and allow the loaf to cool 10 minutes. Unmold, slice, and serve with gravy.

Per serving: 152 calories (17% from fat)
12 g protein; 19 g carbohydrate; 3 g fat; 308 mg sodium; 0 mg cholesterol

Spinach and Mushroom Fritatta

Serves 8

*This fritatta is like a crustless quiche. It is made with silken tofu, which is
available in most grocery stores.*

1	**onion, chopped**
2	**garlic cloves, minced**
2	**cups sliced mushrooms**
1	**10-ounce package frozen spinach, thawed**
1	**10.5-ounce package firm silken tofu**
2	**teaspoons dried basil**
1/2	**teaspoon salt**
1/4	**teaspoon black pepper**
1/4	**teaspoon nutmeg**
1/4	**teaspoon celery seed**
2	**tablespoons couscous**
1/4	**cup soy milk or rice milk**
1	**ripe tomato, thinly sliced**

Heat 1/2 cup of water in a large pot or skillet. Add the onion and garlic
and cook until soft, about 5 minutes. Add the mushrooms and cook
another 5 minutes. Stir in the spinach and cook until the mixture is
very dry.

Preheat the oven to 350°F. In a food processor or blender, process the
tofu until it is very smooth. Rub the basil between the palms of your
hands to crush it, then mix it into the tofu, along with the salt, pepper,
nutmeg, celery seed, couscous and milk.

Add the tofu mixture to the spinach mixture and stir to mix. Pour into a
10-inch pie pan which has been sprayed with a vegetable oil spray.
Bake for 15 minutes, then arrange the sliced tomatoes around the
outside edge. Bake another 10 minutes. Let stand 10 minutes before
serving.

Per serving: 72 calories (12% from fat)
              5 g protein; 11 g carbohydrate;1 g fat; 269 mg sodium; 0 mg cholesterol

Rice and Beans with Greens

Serves 8

If you enjoy simple, down-home food, you'll love this combination of seasoned pinto beans served with brown rice and lightly steamed kale.

Beans: 1 1/2 **cups dry pinto beans**
4 **large garlic cloves, minced**
1 1/2 **teaspoons cumin seed (or 1 teaspoon ground cumin)**
1/2 **teaspoon red pepper flakes**
3/4 **teaspoon salt**

Rinse the beans and soak overnight in about 6 cups of water. Drain and rinse, then place in a pot with 4 cups of water, the garlic, cumin, and red pepper flakes. Simmer until tender, about 1 hour. Add salt to taste.

Rice: 1 **cup brown rice**
1/2 **teaspoon salt**

Bring 4 to 5 cups of water to a boil, then add the salt and rice. Cover loosely and simmer until tender, about 40 minutes. Pour off excess water.

Greens: 1 **bunch kale or collard greens (6 to 8 cups chopped)**
2 **teaspoons soy sauce**
2-3 **garlic cloves, minced**

Wash the greens, remove the stems, and chop the leaves into 1/2-inch wide strips. Heat 1/2 cup of water and the soy sauce in a large pot, then add the garlic and cook 1 minute. Stir in the chopped greens. Cover and cook over medium heat until tender, 3 to 5 minutes.

To serve, place a generous portion of rice on each plate, then top with some of the beans with their liquid. Serve the kale on top of the beans or to the side.

Per serving: 176 calories (6% from fat)
6 g protein; 35 g carbohydrate; 1 g fat; 293 mg sodium; 0 mg cholesterol

Spicy Refried Beans

Serves 8

These beans are delicious, though they aren't actually fried. Serve them with rice and salad, or as a filling for tacos or burritos.

11/2 **cups dry pinto beans**
4   **garlic cloves, minced or crushed**
11/2 **teaspoons cumin**
1/4   **teaspoon cayenne**

1   **onion, chopped**
1   **cup crushed or finely chopped tomatoes**
1   **4-ounce can diced green chilies**
1/2-1 **teaspoon salt**

Clean and rinse the beans, then soak them in about 6 cups of water for 6 to 8 hours. Discard the soaking water, rinse the beans and place them in a large pot with 4 cups of fresh water, the minced garlic, cumin, and cayenne. Simmer until tender, about 1 hour.

Heat 1/2 cup of water in a large skillet. Add the onion and cook until soft, about 5 minutes. Stir in the tomatoes and diced chilies. Cook, uncovered, over medium heat for 10 minutes, stirring occasionally.

Begin adding the cooked beans, along with their liquid, a cup at a time, to the tomato mixture. Mash some of the beans as you add them. When all the beans have been added, stir to mix, then cook over low heat, stirring frequently, until thickened. Add salt to taste.

Per serving: 137 calories (0% from fat)
            7 g protein; 26 g carbohydrate; 0 g fat; 248 mg sodium; 0 mg cholesterol

Quick Chili Beans

Serves 8

There's nothing quite like a bowl of hot chili beans with cornbread to warm up a cold winter day. The addition of Harvest Burger adds hearty flavor and texture to this chili.

2	15-ounce cans pinto beans — OR—
	4 cups cooked pinto beans (see recipe on page 115)
1	15-ounce can tomato sauce
1	4-ounce can diced green chilies
1	cup Harvest Burger for Recipes*
1	tablespoon onion granules or powder
1	teaspoon garlic granules or powder
1	cup corn, fresh, frozen, or canned
1/2	teaspoon cumin

Combine all ingredients in a large saucepan. Cover and simmer over medium-low heat for 15 minutes, stirring occasionally.

Per serving: 116 calories (0% from fat)
        8 g protein; 20 g carbohydrate; 0 g fat; 440 mg sodium; 0 mg cholesterol

* Harvest Burger for Recipes is available in the frozen food section of most supermarkets. You could also use 1/2 cup of textured vegetable protein (TVP) which has been softened with 1/2 cup of boiling water, or 2 to 3 crumbled Boca Burgers. TVP and Boca Burgers are sold in natural food stores.

Chili Corn Pie

Serves 8

This is my idea of comfort food: a savory chili with a delicious cornbread crust. You can use the Quick Chili Beans in the preceding recipe, or two 15-ounce cans of commercially prepared vegetarian chili beans.

- 1 **batch Quick Chili Beans (preceding recipe) — OR —**
- 2 **15-ounce cans fat-free vegetarian chili beans**

- 1½ **cups soy milk**
- 1½ **tablespoons vinegar**

- 1 **cup corn meal**
- 1 **teaspoon baking soda**
- 1/4 **teaspoon salt**

Heat the chili beans, then spread them in a 9 x 9-inch baking dish.

Preheat the oven to 400°F. Mix the soy milk and vinegar and set aside. In a separate bowl, mix the corn meal, baking soda, and salt. Add the soy milk mixture, and stir to remove all lumps. Pour over the hot beans, then bake in the preheated oven until the bread is set and golden brown, about 30 minutes.

Per serving: 264 calories (2% from fat)
14 g protein; 50 g carbohydrate; 1 g fat; 213 mg sodium; 0 mg cholesterol

Truly Terrific Tacos

Makes 12 tacos

These delicious tacos are easy to make with Harvest Burger for Recipes, a meat-like soy product available in the freezer case of most supermarkets. You can also use crumbled Boca Burgers, or any other fat-free vegetarian burgers.

1/2	**onion, chopped**
3	**garlic cloves, crushed**
1	**small green bell pepper, finely diced**
1/2	**cup tomato sauce**
21/2	**cups Harvest Burger for Recipes — OR—**
	4 Boca Burgers, thawed and chopped
2	**teaspoons chili powder**
1/2	**teaspoon cumin**
1/2	**teaspoon oregano**
12	**corn tortillas**
1	**cup shredded romaine lettuce**
1	**medium tomato, diced**
4	**green onions, sliced**

salsa or taco sauce

Heat 1/2 cup of water in a large skillet. Add the onion, garlic and bell pepper and cook until the onion is soft, about 5 minutes. Add the tomato sauce, Harvest Burger or chopped Boca Burger, chili powder, cumin, and oregano. Cook over low heat until the mixture is fairly dry.

Place a small amount of filling on a tortilla in a heavy, ungreased skillet. Heat until the tortilla is warm and pliable then fold it in half and cook on each side for 60 seconds or longer for a crisper taco. Garnish with remaining ingredients.

Per taco: 114 calories (8% from fat)
          7 g protein; 19 g carbohydrate; 1 g fat; 86 mg sodium; 0 mg cholesterol

Quick Bean Burritos

Makes 4 burritos

Burritos make a quick, tasty, and very portable meal which can be eaten hot or cold. Fat-Free refried beans are available in most markets. A growing number of markets also carry fat-free flour tortillas.

1	**15-ounce can fat-free refried beans, heated**
4	**flour tortillas (preferably fat-free)**
1-2	**cups shredded romaine lettuce**
2-3	**tomatoes, diced or cut into wedges**
3	**green onions, sliced**
1	**cup salsa**

Heat a tortilla in a large, ungreased skillet until it is warm and soft. Spread a line of the heated beans down the center of the tortilla, then top with lettuce, tomato, onions, and salsa. Fold the bottom end toward the center, then roll the tortilla around the filling. Repeat with remaining tortillas.

Per burrito: 300 calories (10% from fat)
              12 g protein; 55 g carbohydrate; 3 g fat; 196 mg sodium; 0 mg cholesterol

Burgers and Hot Dogs

Several excellent fat-free burgers and hot dogs are available in natural food stores and in many supermarkets. Check the deli case as well as the freezer section of your store, and if you can't find them, ask the manager to order them. Some of the ones we've tried and liked include:

Boca Burgers (Boca Burger Company)
Natural Touch Vegan Burger (Worthington Foods)
Yves Veggie Burger (Yves Fine Foods)
Yves Veggie Wieners (Yves Fine Foods)
Light Burgers (Lightlife Foods)
Smart Dogs (Lightlife Foods)

Pita Pizzas

Makes 6 pizzas

Pita bread makes a perfect crust for individual pizzas. Serve Pita Pizzas for quick meals or for snacks. You can make them almost instantly if you keep some pizza sauce and chopped vegetables in the refrigerator.

1	15-ounce can tomato sauce
1	6-ounce can tomato paste
1	teaspoon garlic granules or powder
1/2	teaspoon each: basil, oregano, and thyme
2	green onions, thinly sliced
1	green or red bell pepper, diced
1	cup thinly sliced mushrooms
6	pieces of pita bread

Preheat the oven to 375°F.

Combine the tomato sauce, tomato paste, garlic granules and herbs for the sauce.

Prepare the vegetables as directed.

For each pizza, turn a piece of pita bread upside down and spread it with some of the sauce. Top liberally with chopped vegetables. Place on a cookie sheet and bake until the edges are lightly browned, about 10 minutes.

Note: You will only need about half the sauce for 6 pizzas. Refrigerate or freeze the remainder for use at another time.

Per pizza: 185 calories (10% from fat)
        7 g protein; 35 g carbohydrate; 2 g fat; 337 mg sodium; 0 mg cholesterol

Middle Eastern Lentils and Rice

Serves 8

This traditional Middle Eastern dish is topped with a crisp green salad and tart lemon vinaigrette. The combination is simply delicious.

1	tablespoon soy sauce
2	large onions, coarsely chopped
1	cup lentils, rinsed
1	cup brown rice
4	cups boiling water
1 1/2	teaspoons salt

4-6	cups prewashed salad mix or torn leaf lettuce
1-2	tomatoes
1/2	cucumber, thinly sliced

3	tablespoons lemon juice
2	tablespoons seasoned rice vinegar
1	garlic clove, pressed
1	teaspoon sugar or other sweetener
1/2	teaspoon paprika
1/4	teaspoon dry mustard
1/4	teaspoon salt

Heat 1/4 cup of water and the soy sauce in a large pot. Add the onions and cook, stirring occasionally, until they are soft and begin to brown. This will take about 10 minutes. Add the lentils, rice, boiling water, and salt. Bring to a simmer, then cover and cook over medium heat until the lentils and rice are tender, about 50 minutes. Stir occasionally and add additional water if the mixture begins to stick.

While the lentil mixture is cooking, prepare a generous green salad, using salad mix or leaf lettuce, tomatoes, cucumber, and any other ingredients you enjoy in a salad. Mix the remaining ingredients for the dressing. Dress the salad just before serving. To serve, place a portion of lentil mixture on each plate and top with a generous serving of salad.

Per serving: 194 calories (3% from fat)
            8 g protein; 38 g carbohydrate; 1 g fat; 550 mg sodium; 0 mg cholesterol

Hungarian Goulash

Serves 8

This is a perfect "make-ahead" recipe, as it is actually tastier the second day. It is made with seitan ("say-tan"), a high-protein wheat product which has a meaty taste and texture. Seitan is sold in natural food stores. If you are unable to locate seitan, you can use a cup of Harvest Burger for Recipes in its place.

1	large onion
2	tablespoons soy sauce
3	cups sliced mushrooms
1	large red bell pepper, diced
2	celery stalks, sliced
3	tablespoons minced garlic (about 10 large cloves)
8	ounces seitan, cut into slices — OR—
	1 cup Harvest Burger for Recipes
1	12-ounce jar water-packed roasted red peppers
1/2	cup ketchup
2	tablespoons minced fresh basil — OR—
	2 teaspoons dried basil
1	teaspoon paprika
1/4	teaspoon black pepper
1	8-ounce package of fettucine, rotini, or other pasta

Cut the onion in half, then into thin crescents. Heat 1/2 cup of water and the soy sauce in a large skillet. Add the onion and cook over high heat, stirring often, until the water has evaporated. Add an additional 1/2 cup of water, along with the mushrooms, bell pepper, celery, and garlic. Continue cooking over medium heat for 8 to 10 minutes, then stir in the sliced seitan (or Harvest Burger for Recipes).

Use a food processor or blender to puree the roasted red peppers, including any liquid. Add to the vegetables along with the ketchup, basil, paprika, pepper, and 1 cup of water. Cover and simmer 10 minutes.

Cook the pasta in boiling water until it is tender. Rinse and drain, then spread on a platter. Top with the goulash and serve.

Per serving: 140 calories (0% from fat)
9 g protein; 25 g carbohydrate; 0 g fat; 254 mg sodium; 0 mg cholesterol

Polenta with Hearty BBQ Sauce

Serves 6

Harvest Burger for Recipes, a fat-free soy product, adds flavor, texture, and protein to this tasty barbecue sauce which is delicious with polenta.

1   **cup polenta**
1/2-1 **teaspoon salt**

1   **large onion, chopped**
2   **large garlic cloves, minced**
1   **red or green bell pepper, finely diced**
1   **cup Harvest Burger for Recipes — OR—**
       1 cup textured vegetable protein +1 cup water — OR—
       2-3 Boca Burgers, thawed and chopped
1   **15-ounce can tomato sauce or crushed tomatoes**
1   **tablespoon sugar or other sweetener**
2-3   **teaspoons chili powder**
1   **teaspoon garlic granules or powder**
2   **tablespoons cider vinegar**
1-2   **tablespoons soy sauce**
1   **teaspoon stoneground mustard**

Combine the polenta and salt with 5 cups of water in a pan. Simmer, uncovered, stirring frequently, until very thick, 15 to 20 minutes.

In the meantime, heat 1/2 cup of water in a large pot or skillet, then add the onion, garlic, and bell pepper. Cook until the onion is soft, about 5 minutes. Add the remaining ingredients and another 1/2 cup of water. Cook over medium heat, stirring frequently, for about 10 minutes. To serve, spread some cooked polenta onto a plate or into a bowl, and top with the sauce.

Per serving: 175 calories (0% from fat)
          10 g protein; 31g carbohydrate; 0 g fat; 320-497 mg sodium; 0 mg cholesterol

Variation: Spread the cooked polenta in a baking dish to a depth of about 1/2-inch and chill completely. Cut the chilled polenta into squares and grill or saute in an oil-sprayed nonstick skillet. Top with sauce.

Curried Mushrooms and Chickpeas

Serves 8

This Indian dish is spicy and delicious with rice or couscous. You can make it milder, if desired, by decreasing the amount of cayenne.

2	**large onions, chopped**
11/2	**tablespoons cumin seeds**
11/2	**pounds mushrooms, sliced**
1	**28-ounce can crushed tomatoes**
1	**15-ounce can garbanzo beans, drained**
1	**teaspoon turmeric**
1	**teaspoon coriander**
1/2	**teaspoon cayenne**
1/2	**teaspoon ginger**

Heat 1/2 cup of water in a large pot and add the onions. Cook until soft, about 5 minutes, then add the cumin seed and mushrooms.
Continue cooking over medium heat until mushroom are light brown, about 10 minutes. Add the tomatoes, garbanzo beans, and spices.
Cook 30 minutes or longer, until the mushrooms are tender and the flavors are well blended.

Per serving: 116 calories (8% from fat)
5 g protein; 20 g carbohydrate; 1 g fat; 286 mg sodium; 0 mg cholesterol

SWEETS

Berry Cobbler

Serves 9

The "birth" of this recipe marked the end of my berry pie-making days.
It is so much easier to make, is fat-free, and tastes absolutely wonderful.

Berry mixture:

5-6	**cups fresh or frozen berries (boysenberries, blackberries, raspberries, or a mixture of these)**
3	**tablespoons whole wheat pastry flour**
1/2	**cup sugar**

Topping:

1	**cup whole wheat pastry flour**
2	**tablespoons sugar**
1 1/2	**teaspoons baking powder**
1/4	**teaspoon salt**
2/3	**cup soy milk or rice milk**

Spread the berries in a 9 x 9-inch baking dish and mix in 3 tablespoons of flour and 1/2 cup of sugar. Place them in the oven and turn it on to 375°F. Leave the berries in the oven until they are hot, for about 15 minutes.

While the berries are heating, prepare the topping. Mix 1 cup of flour and 2 tablespoons of sugar with the baking powder and salt. Add the soy milk or rice milk and stir until the batter is smooth. Spread evenly over the hot berries (don't worry if they're not completely covered), then bake until golden brown, 25 to 30 minutes.

Per serving: 152 calories (0% from fat)
3 g. protein; 34 g carbohydrate; 0 g fat; 68 mg sodium; 0 mg cholesterol

Cranberry Apple Crisp

Serves 8

This fat-free dessert is colorful and easy to prepare. Most stores carry dried cranberries. Be sure to buy the variety without added fat.

2	**large, tart apples, peeled and sliced**
1/2	**cup dried cranberries**
3/4	**cup rolled oats**
3/4	**cup Grape-Nuts Cereal**
1/2	**teaspoon cinnamon**
1/3	**cup maple syrup**
2/3	**cup apple juice**
1/4	**teaspoon cornstarch or arrowroot**

Preheat the oven to 350°F. Spread the apples in a 9 x 9-inch baking dish. Sprinkle with cranberries.

In a mixing bowl, stir the rolled oats, Grape-Nuts, and cinnamon together, then add the maple syrup and mix thoroughly. Distribute evenly over apple-cranberry mixture.

Mix apple juice with cornstarch or arrowroot, stirring to remove any lumps. Pour evenly over other ingredients. Bake for 45 minutes, or until the apples are tender.

Per serving: 139 calories (4% from fat)
2.5 g protein; 31 g carbohydrate; 1 g fat; 74 mg sodium; 0 mg cholesterol

Gingerbread

One 9 x 9-inch cake

This gingerbread contains no added fat, yet it is moist and delicious. Try serving it with hot applesauce for a real treat.

1/2	**cup raisins**
1/2	**cup pitted dates, chopped**
13/4	**cups water**
3/4	**cup sugar**
1/2	**teaspoon salt**
2	**teaspoons cinnamon**
1	**teaspoon ginger**
3/4	**teaspoon nutmeg**
1/4	**teaspoon cloves**
2	**cups whole wheat pastry flour**
1	**teaspoon baking soda**
1	**teaspoon baking powder**

Combine the raisins, dates, water, sugar, salt and spices in a large saucepan and bring to a boil. Boil for 2 minutes, then remove from heat and cool completely (this is important).

Preheat the oven to 350°F. Stir the flour, baking soda and baking powder together. Add to the cooled fruit mixture and stir to mix. Spread into a 9 x 9-inch pan which has been sprayed with a nonstick spray and bake for 30 minutes, or until a toothpick inserted into the center comes out clean.

Per serving: 207 calories (0% from fat);
         4 g protein; 48 g carbohydrate; 0 g fat; 216 mg sodium; 0 mg cholesterol

Banana Cake

Serves 9

My dear friend Lee West is a wonderful man and a fabulous cook. He took this recipe from my other, The Peaceful Palate, and made it deliciously fat-free.

2	**cups whole wheat pastry flour**
1	**cup raw wheat germ**
2	**teaspoons baking soda**
1/2	**teaspoon salt**
4	**ripe bananas, mashed (about 21/2 cups)**
1/2	**cup sugar**
3/4	**cup soy milk or rice milk**
1	**teaspoon vanilla**
1/3	**cup raisins or chopped dates**

powdered sugar for dusting (optional)

Preheat the oven to 350°F. Mix the flour, wheat germ, soda, and salt in a mixing bowl.

In another mixing bowl, mash the bananas and mix in the sugar, milk and vanilla. Add the flour mixture, along with the raisins or dates, and stir to mix.

Spread into an oil-sprayed 9 x 9-inch pan, and bake for 55 minutes, until a toothpick inserted into the center comes out clean.

Dust with powdered sugar if desired.

Per serving: 240 calories (7% from fat)
8 g protein; 48 g carbohydrate; 2 g fat; 303 mg sodium; 0 mg cholesterol

Pumpkin Raisin Cookies

Makes 36 3-inch cookies

These plump, moist cookies are easy to make and delicious.

3   **cups whole wheat pastry flour**
3/4   **cup sugar**
4   **teaspoons baking powder**
1   **teaspoon baking soda**
1   **teaspoon salt**
2   **teaspoons cinnamon**
1/2   **teaspoon nutmeg**

1   **15-ounce can solid-pack pumpkin (about 2 cups)**
1/2   **cup molasses**
1   **cup soy milk, rice milk, or water**
1   **cup raisins**

Preheat the oven to 350°F. Mix the dry ingredients together in one bowl, and the pumpkin, molasses, milk or water in another. Combine the two mixtures, then stir in the raisins.

Drop by tablespoonfuls onto a baking sheet which has been lightly oil-sprayed. Bake 15 minutes, until lightly browned. Remove from baking sheet with a spatula, and place on a rack to cool. Once cooled, store in an airtight container in the refrigerator.

Per cookie: 80 calories (0% from fat)
             2 g protein; 18 g carbohydrate; 0 g fat;110 mg sodium; 0 mg cholesterol

Pumpkin Pie

One 9-inch pie

This is a fat-free version of the traditional favorite.

- 1 **cup Grape-Nuts cereal**
- 1/4 **cup apple juice concentrate (undiluted)**

- 5 **tablespoons cornstarch**
- 1/2 **cup sugar**
- 1/2 **teaspoon salt**
- 1 **teaspoon cinnamon**
- 1/2 **teaspoon ginger**
- 1/8 **teaspoon cloves**
- 1 **15-ounce can pumpkin**
- 1 1/2 **cups soy milk or rice milk**

Preheat the oven to 350°F. Mix the Grape-Nuts and apple juice concentrate, then pat into the bottom and part way up the sides of a 9-inch pie pan. Bake 7 minutes. Remove from the oven and set aside. Leave the oven set to 350°F.

In a large bowl combine the cornstarch with the sugar, salt, cinnamon, ginger, and cloves. Blend in the pumpkin and milk. Pour into the baked crust and bake 45 minutes. Cool before cutting.

Per serving: 150 calories 0% from fat)
         3 g protein; 33 g carbohydrate; 0 g fat;186 mg sodium; 0 mg cholesterol

Banana Dream Pie

One 9-inch pie

You won't believe this heavenly pie!

1	**cup Grape-Nuts cereal**
1/4	**cup apple juice concentrate (undiluted)**
1/2	**cup sugar**
6	**tablespoons cornstarch**
2	**cups soy milk or rice milk**
1/2	**teaspoon salt**
1	**teaspoon vanilla**
1/2	**pound firm tofu**
2	**ripe bananas**

Preheat the oven to 350°F. Mix the Grape-Nuts and apple juice concentrate, then pat into the bottom and part way up the sides of a 9-inch pie pan. Bake until edges just begin to darken, about 8 minutes. Cool.

Mix the sugar and cornstarch in a saucepan, then stir in the milk and salt. Cook over medium heat, stirring constantly, until the mixture becomes a very thick pudding. Remove from heat and stir in the vanilla.

Drain the tofu and blend it in a food processor until it is totally smooth, then add it to the pudding and blend until smooth.

Slice the bananas into thin rounds over the cooled crust. Spread the pudding mixture on top. Refrigerate until completely chilled, at least two hours.

Per serving: 204 calories (9% from fat)
6 g protein; 42 g carbohydrate; 1 g fat; 255 mg sodium; 0 mg cholesterol

Tofu Cheesecake

One 9-inch pie

This velvety "cheesecake," is made with agar flakes, which are traditional in Japanese cooking. Look for them in natural food stores or Asian markets.

1	**cup Grape-Nuts cereal or fat-free granola**
1/4	**cup apple juice concentrate (undiluted)**

Preheat the oven to 350°F. Mix the Grape-Nuts (or granola) and apple juice concentrate. Pat into a 9-inch pie pan. Bake for 8 minutes. Cool.

2	**tablespoons agar flakes**
2/3	**cup soy milk or rice milk**
1/2	**cup sugar**
1/2	**teaspoon salt**
2	**teaspoons grated lemon rind**
4	**tablespoons lemon juice**
2	**teaspoons vanilla**
1	**pound firm tofu**

Combine the agar, milk, sugar and salt. Let stand 5 minutes, then bring to a simmer over low heat. Cook, stirring often for 5 minutes. Pour into a blender, and add the lemon rind, lemon juice, vanilla, and tofu. Blend until very smooth. Spread evenly over the cooled crust.

1/3	**cup sugar**
1 1/2	**tablespoons cornstarch**
1 1/2	**tablespoons lemon juice**
1/2	**teaspoon grated lemon rind**
1/3	**cup water**
2	**cups fresh berries, kiwi slices, mandarin oranges, etc.**

Combine the sugar, cornstarch, lemon juice, lemon rind, and water in a saucepan and whisk smooth. Heat, stirring constantly, until clear and thick. Spread over cheesecake. Top with fresh fruit. Chill thoroughly.

Per serving: 192 calories (9% from fat)
8 g protein; 36 g carbohydrate; 2 g fat; 247 mg sodium; 0 mg cholesterol

Chocolate Torte

Serves 12

This torte is pure chocolate decadence. It tastes unbelievably rich, yet is surprisingly low in fat.

In a medium saucepan, stir together the following ingredients:

1	**cup couscous**
1	**cup sugar**
1/4	**cup cocoa**
1/4	**teaspoon salt**
2 1/2	**cups water**

Bring to a simmer and cook over medium heat until thickened, about 7 minutes. Spread in the bottom of an ungreased 9-inch springform pan.

In another pan, combine the following ingredients:

1/2	**cup sugar**
5	**tablespoons cornstarch**
3	**tablespoons cocoa**
2	**cups soy milk**

Whisk smooth, then cook over medium heat, stirring constantly until a very thick pudding forms. Spread evenly over the top of the couscous mixture.

Chill completely before serving.

Per serving: 161 calories (5% from fat)
           2.5 g protein; 36 g carbohydrate; 1 g fat; 106 mg sodium; 0 mg cholesterol

Tropical Freeze

Serves 3

Pureed frozen fruit makes a wonderful dessert, without the fat or refined sugar of ice cream. Look for frozen mango pieces in your supermarket, or you can make your own using fresh mangoes. To freeze bananas, peel and break into chunks. Place them loosely in a covered container in the freezer.

1   orange, peeled
1   cup frozen banana chunks
1   cup frozen mango chunks
1/2-1 cup soy milk or rice milk

Cut the orange in half and remove any seeds, then place in a blender with the remaining ingredients and process until thick and very smooth.

Per serving: 152 calories (5% from fat)
          2 g protein; 33 g carbohydrate; 1 g fat; 24 mg sodium; 0 mg cholesterol

Banana Date Shake

Serves 2

Bananas are easy to freeze and make a thick and creamy shake. Just peel them and break them into pieces. Place them loosely in a covered container in the freezer.

1/2   cup soy milk or rice milk
4-6   pitted dates
2   cups frozen banana chunks

Place the milk and dates into a blender and blend until the dates are in very small pieces. Add the bananas and blend until thick and smooth.

Per serving: 143 calories (6% from fat)
          3 g protein; 30 g carbohydrate; 1 g fat; 46 mg sodium; 0 mg cholesterol

Quick Rice Pudding

Serves 4

1 1/2 **cups soy milk (vanilla or plain)**
1   **tablespoon cornstarch**
2   **cups cooked rice (brown or white)**
1/4   **cup maple syrup**
1/3   **cup raisins**
1/4   **teaspoon cinnamon**
1   **teaspoon vanilla**

Combine the soy milk and cornstarch in a medium-sized saucepan and stir to remove any lumps. Add the rice, maple syrup, raisins and cinnamon and bring to a simmer over medium heat. Cook 3 minutes, then remove from heat and stir in vanilla. Serve hot or cold.

Per serving: 151 calories (6% from fat)
          2.5 g protein; 34 g carbohydrate; 1 g fat; 28 mg sodium; 0 mg cholesterol

Chocolate Tofu Pudding

Serves 2

Silken tofu has a much smoother texture than regular tofu, making it ideal as a base for puddings. Mori Nu is one brand which is sold in most grocery stores.

1   **10.5-ounce package firm silken tofu**
1   **tablespoon cocoa**
1/2   **teaspoon salt**
1/3   **cup maple syrup or sugar**
1   **teaspoon vanilla**

Place all ingredients into a food processor or blender and blend until completely smooth. Spoon into small bowls and chill before serving.

Per serving: 296 calories (13% from fat)
          16 g protein; 48 g carbohydrate; 4 g fat; 282 mg sodium; 0 mg cholesterol

Lemon Pudding

Serves 2

1   **10.5-ounce package firm silken tofu**
1   **tablespoon lemon peel**
1/3   **cup + 1 tablespoon sugar or other sweetener**
1/4   **cup lemon juice**
1/4   **teaspoon salt**
pinch turmeric (optional)

Place all ingredients into a food processor or blender and blend until completely smooth. Spoon into two bowls and chill.

Per serving: 256 calories (13% from fat)
                        10 g protein; 45 g carbohydrate; 4 g fat; 337 mg sodium; 0 mg cholesterol

Blueberry Pudding

Serves 2

1   **10.5-ounce package firm silken tofu**
1   **cup blueberries, fresh or frozen**
2   **tablespoons lemon juice**
1/3   **cup sugar or other sweetener**
1/4   **teaspoon salt**

Place all ingredients into a food processor or blender and blend until completely smooth. Spoon into two bowls and chill.

Per serving: 254 calories (13% from fat)
                        10 g protein; 44 g carbohydrate; 4 g fat; 341 mg sodium; 0 mg cholesterol

Chocolate Pudding

Serves 4

This is delicious, old-fashioned chocolate pudding.

- 2   **cups soy milk or rice milk**
- 3   **tablespoons cocoa**
- 5   **tablespoons cornstarch or arrowroot**
- 1/2   **cup sugar**
- 1   **teaspoon vanilla**

Whisk all the ingredients together in a saucepan until all the lumps are dissolved. Cook over medium heat, stirring constantly until the pudding is very thick. Pour into individual serving dishes and chill.

Prune Whip

Serves 4

Try this before you laugh, because it really tastes good. Carob powder is available in natural food stores and some supermarkets.

- 1   **cup pitted prunes**

- 1/3   **cup soy milk**
- 3   **tablespoons carob powder**
- 2   **tablespoons maple syrup**

Combine the prunes and 1 cup of water in a saucepan. Cover and simmer until the prunes are tender, about 20 minutes. Cool slightly, then transfer the prunes, including any liquid, into a blender. Add the remaining ingredients and blend until completely smooth. Spoon into small serving dishes and chill.

Per serving: 166 calories (0% from fat)
          2 g protein; 39 g carbohydrate; 0 g fat; 12 mg sodium; 0 mg cholesterol

Creamy Prune Pudding

Serves 4

Silken tofu makes this pudding creamy as well as nutritious.

- 1 **cup stewed prunes, pitted (page 37)**
- 1 **10.5-ounce package firm silken tofu**
- 1/4 **cup sugar**
- 1 **teaspoon vanilla**
- 1/2 **teaspoon lemon juice**
- 1/4 **teaspoon salt**

Place all the ingredients into a food processor or blender and blend until completely smooth. Spoon into small serving dishes and chill.

Per serving: 147 calories (12% from fat)
6 g protein; 26 g carbohydrate; 2 g fat; 169 mg sodium; 0 mg cholesterol

Holiday Fruit Bread

Makes 2 loaves (40 slices)

This delicioius holiday bread can be easily modified by using different combinations of dried fruit.

11/2 **cups soy or rice milk**
2   **tablespoons vinegar**

2   **cups whole wheat flour**
1   **cup unbleached flour**
2   **teaspoons baking soda**
1/2   **teaspoon salt**
1/4   **cup molasses**
1/3   **cup maple syrup**
1   **cup dark raisins**
1   **cup chopped dried figs**
1   **cup golden raisins**
1/2   **cup chopped pitted dates**
1/2   **cup chopped dried apricots**

Preheat the oven to 325°F.   Mix the milk and vinegar and set aside.

In a large bowl, mix the flours, soda, and salt. Add the milk-vinegar mixture, molasses, and maple syrup. Mix well, then stir in the dried fruit. Divide the batter between two oil-sprayed loaf pans and bake for one hour.

Per slice: 101 calories (0% from fat)
            2 g protein; 23 g carbohydrate; 0 g fat; 75 mg sodium; 0 mg cholesterol

Indian Pudding

Serves 4

You'll love this delicious, traditional New England dessert.

1/2	**cup cornmeal**
31/2	**cups soy milk**
1	**tablespoon molasses**
1/4	**cup maple syrup**
1/4	**teaspoon salt**
1	**teaspoon ginger**
1/2	**teaspoon cinnamon**

In a heavy saucepan, combine the cornmeal and 3 cups of the soy milk. Bring to a simmer, then cook over medium heat, stirring frequently, for 5 minutes. Stir in the molasses, maple syrup, salt, and spices. Continue cooking another 10 minutes, stirring often. Pour into a baking dish, then add the remaining 1/2 cup of milk, stirring to just barely mix. Bake at 350°F for 30 minutes. Turn off the oven. Leave the pudding in the oven with door closed another 30 minutes. Serve warm or cold.

Per serving: 147 calories (9% from fat)
   4 g protein; 30 g carbohydrate; 2 g fat; 155 mg sodium; 0 mg cholesterol

Ginger Peachy Bread Pudding

Serves 9

1	28-ounce can sliced peaches
1	tablespoon cornstarch
6	cups cubed whole grain bread (about 8 slices)
13/4	cups soy milk or rice milk
1/3	cup packed brown sugar
3/4	cup golden raisins
1/2	teaspoon ginger
1/2	teaspoon cinnamon
1/4	teaspoon nutmeg
1/4	teaspoon salt
1	teaspoon vanilla
1/4	cup finely chopped crystallized ginger (optional)
2	tablespoons brown sugar

Drain the liquid from the peaches into a large mixing bowl and mix it with the cornstarch. Stir to dissolve any lumps, then add the bread cubes, soy or rice milk, brown sugar, raisins, ginger, cinnamon, nutmeg, salt, and vanilla. Mix well. Stir in the crystallized ginger if desired. Chop the peaches and stir them into the mixture. Spread in a 9 x 9-inch baking dish, then sprinkle the top with brown sugar and let stand 5 minutes while the oven preheats to 350°F. Bake for 35 minutes. Serve warm or cooled.

Per serving: 252 calories (4% from fat)
3 g protein; 57 g carbohydrate; 1 g fat; 185 mg sodium; 0 mg cholesterol

Baked Apples

Serves 4

These baked apples make a great dessert and you can even eat them for breakfast!

> 4   **tart apples**
> 5-7 **pitted dates, chopped**
> 1/2 **teaspoon cinnamon**

Wash the apples, then remove the core to within 1/4-inch of the bottoms. Combine the dates and cinnamon, then distribute equally into each of the apples. Place in a baking dish filled with 1/4 inch of hot water, and bake at 350°F for 40 to 60 minutes. Serve warm or cold.

Per apple: 124 calories (0% from fat)
0.5 g protein; 30 g carbohydrate; 0 g fat; 0 mg sodium; 0 mg cholesterol

Poached Pears

Serves 4

Poached pears are attractive, delicious, and deceptively easy to prepare.

> 2   **large ripe pears**
> 1/2 **cup apple juice concentrate**
> 1/2 **cup white wine or water**
> 1   **bag Celestial Seasonings Harvest Spice tea — OR—**
>   1/2 **teaspoon cinnamon**

Peel the pears, cut them in half, and remove the cores. Place the pears in a saucepan with the remaining ingredients. Simmer until tender when pierced with a fork, 15 to 20 minutes. Remove the pears from the pan and place in serving dishes. Remove the tea bag from the pan, then boil the juice until it is quite thick, about 5 minutes. Pour it over the pears.

Per serving: 135 calories (0% from fat)
1 g protein; 31 g carbohydrate; 0 g fat; 13 mg sodium; 0 mg cholesterol

INDEX

photograph by Brooke Raymond

About the Author

Jennifer Raymond is a popular cooking and nutrition instructor throughout the United States. She has worked as a nutrition specialist and guest chef with Dean Ornish, M.D., in his "Open Your Heart" program for the prevention and reversal of heart disease. While working with the patients in this program, she became aware of the need for fat-free recipes that could be prepared quickly and easily, with readily available ingredients. As she developed and shared these recipes, the patients in the program encouraged her to compile them into a book. The result is *Fat-Free & Easy*.

Jennifer lives in Calistoga, California with her husband and five dogs. She enjoys hiking, bicycle riding, gardening, and of course, cooking!